Giorgio Piola

Formula 1
technical analysis 2005 2006

CW00926551

THE 2005 SEASON

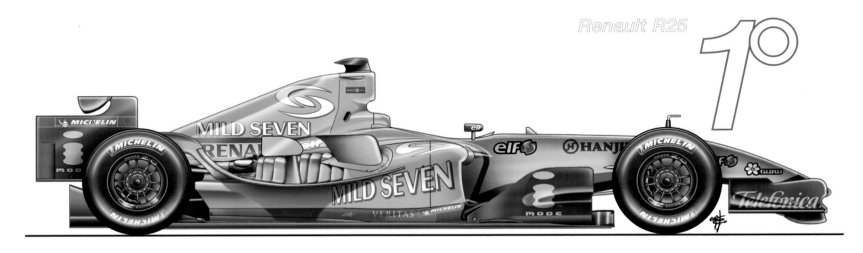

Renault R25

The domination of Ferrari, which lasted six consecutive seasons and yielded six world constructors' titles for Maranello and five drivers' for Michael Schumacher, came to a brusque end in 2005. The season turned out to be a duel between Renault and McLaren-Mercedes and, as they both used Michelin tyres, they battled it out on equal terms. The surprise was that Ferrari was out of the fight, having only won the one race at Indianapolis, an unusual event that saw the complete and forced withdrawal of all the teams using the French tyres. Even though its products had returned the best yield throughout the whole season in relation to its rival Bridgestone, Michelin had underestimated the safety aspect for the American track and arrived there with tyres that could not withstand the stress of the banked turns of the legendary Indiana bowl. The obligation decreed by the regulations to use a single tyre for the whole race conditioned the season, with Michelin finding itself with a clear advantage in relation to its Japanese opposition, transforming that which was a considerable strongpoint for Ferrari into a severe handicap. Yet the regulation that imposed the use of a single engine for two races did not have much influence on the progress of the season, penalising more the McLarens than the Renaults, which had more powerful but especially more reliable engines than those of Mercedes-Benz.

RENAULT'S FIRST WORLD CHAMPIONSHIP

So the battle between Renault and McLaren took place on equal terms, ensuring the two teams forgot the freak problems of previous years, McLaren, competing with the disappointing MP4-18 of 2003 – the only car in the history of modern Formula One that was never able to make its championship debut – and the MP4-19; Renault held back in 2004 by a car it was difficult to take to the limit and not very reliable. And it was reliability that enabled Fernando Alonso to prevail over his rival Kimi Raikkonen and permitted the Renault R25 to snatch the Constructors' title from the McLaren MP4-20 – certainly less reliable, but in many ways showing itself to be superior in terms of pure performance - at the last race of the season in China. Too many engine failures marked Raikkonen's season, often forcing him into a recovery kind of race, while Alonso was able to rely on his power unit – the only one with a 72° V compared to the 90° of the opposition – designed under the direction of Rob White and one that confirmed it was the best engine of the season in terms of performance and reliability. In that decisive race at Shanghai, Renault even technically overtook Mercedes-Benz by presenting a specific "E" of its 10 cylinder, which was more powerful than that of its German rival.

RENAULT AND McLAREN: TWO WINNING AND REVOLUTIONARY CARS

The two top cars of the 2005 season were both direct descendents of their predecessors, respectively the Renault R24 of a year earlier and the "B" version of the McLaren-Mercedes-Benz MP4-19, which first appeared in France. The two camps went for the extreme development of their aerodynamics, even if both their overall shape and that of a number of components were very different from each other.

Characterised by a longer wheelbase and a different weight distribution, the R25 was of rounder shape and had a different fluidynamics arrangement in the side pods, with the introduction of a series of vents in the upper part of the sidepods: apart from dissipating heat, they also improved the efficiency of the air flow towards the rear area. The car also had large chimneys that functioned more than anything else purely aerodynamically, having been used in the closed version.

After long discussions on the advantages of the twin keel for the front suspension mounts, first used by Sauber, each dominating team chose a different path. They did not adopt either a single or double keel but chose extremely innovative but different layouts for the suspension's wishbone mounts. The R25 used a V-shaped tubular structure that offered the same structural advantages as the central bulb, but with the addition of a better quality of air flow in that zone, which is especially critical to lower aerodynamics. The MP4-20

went back almost completely to the split lateral mounts in the lower part of the chassis, which were introduced by Jean-Claude Migeot on the 1990 Tyrrell 019.

THE TOYOTA BOOM
Immediately behind the three top teams came Toyota, finally able to consolidate the enormous effort of the previous two seasons with a car that took the Japanese giant to its first much deserved podium places. When it made its debut, the TF105 was not especially impressive, but the enormous number of small modifications carried out by the group of technicians led by Mike Gascoyne transformed the Toyota into a competitive and reliable car right from the first race in Australia. The team was the only one to introduce a laboratory car - a modified version of the TF105 - for the last two races of the season to develop its new contender for the 2006 season.
The debut of Red Bull, which had risen from the ashes of the 2004 Jaguar team, was also positive and was able to move into the spotlight, often as a result of the difficulties experienced by its opposing teams.

THE DISAPPOINTMENTS
OF THE SEASON
The umpteenth disappointment for Williams-BMW culminated in divorce between the British team and the German giant, which decided to take the plunge and join the Circus with its own team from 2006 by buying Sauber.

There was also considerable disappointment at BAR-Honda, because the team fell from second place in the Constructors' championship in 2004 to seventh at the end of 2005. The year was peppered with many technical and reliability problems, made worse by the Federation's discovery of the double fuel tank, which earned the team disqualification the day after the Grand Prix of San Marino. This drastic action not only stopped the Anglo-Japanese team from competing in two Grands Prix, but it still severely influenced BAR-Honda's continuation of the season.

THE ABSURDITY OF INDIANAPOLIS
The obligation to use a single set of tyres over the full duration of the race not only had severe repercussions on the progress of the season, with Bridgestone way behind its rival Michelin, but constituted the premise for one of the darkest pages in the history of modern F1. That was, of course, the Indianapolis affair, in which only six cars lined up on the grid for the start, all of them on Bridgestone tyres. A real disgrace for the French manufacturer, which was guilty of having brought tyres to the Brickyard that were not able to cover the full race distance there and immediately created a crisis, causing a chain of accidents in practice.

FAREWELL MINARDI AND JORDAN
The 2005 season will also be remembered as the last for two teams, Minardi and Jordan. The Italian team entered Formula One back in 1985 and, despite the fact that it has always

been afflicted with problems linked to its annual budget, made a notable technical contribution to the category, often introducing new developments that were then taken up by other teams the following year.
If nothing else, credit should be given to Jordan for having given Michael Schumacher his F1 debut at the 1991 Grand Prix of Belgium. At the time, the team was running a very interesting car designed by Gary Anderson, whose career in Formula One brought legendary changes, having gradually transformed himself from Emerson Fittipaldi's chief mechanic on the McLaren M23 into one of the best established designers in the Circus.
In reality, both Minardi and Jordan only left the world championship in name, because both are still competing in the 2006 season. The former was acquired by Red Bull and named Toro Rosso, the latter Midland.
This analysis of the 2005 F1 season includes not only contributions from engineers Mauro Forghieri and Mauro Coppini on power units, Kazuiko Kawai, Mark Hughes and James Allen on tyres and strategies, there is also a table by Michele Merlino on the use of engines by the various teams during the season, which highlights the numerous problems experienced by the teams over the 19 Grands Prix of the year.

Ferrari F2004 M 3°

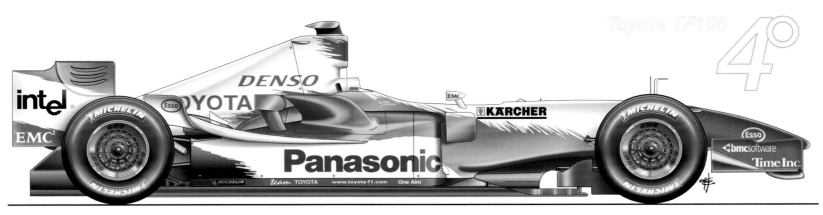

Toyota TF105 4°

Williams FW27 5°

BAR 007 6°

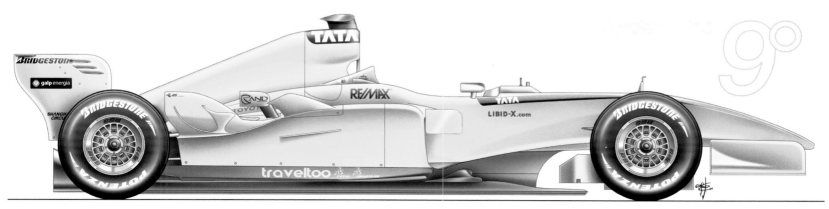

CHASSIS HISTORY

This chapter of the Technical Analysis has been subjected to penalisation: as well as being the third season in which cars were obliged to enter parc fermé between qualifying and the race, the freezing of set-ups and the elimination of the warm up, 2005 was a year in which new regulations were introduced: the obligation to maintain the same engine for two consecutive races, with a penalty of being dropped back 10 places on the grid if the power unit was changed before a race. These harsh limitations meant a drastic reduction in the use of the spare car, with most of the teams no longer bringing a fourth chassis to the circuits as a reserve to be assembled in the case of an accident.

The spare was only used in cases of real necessity and upon the authorisation of the marshals.

The rule in this case was the same as in 2004: once the spare car had been used it would become, to all intents and purposes, the team's race car without the possibility of returning to the original.

Having made that clear, we decided to reduce the space set aside for the chassis illustrations and dedicate it only to the first four teams in the constructors' classification.

The Ferrari graphics are especially substantial, given that Maranello once more fielded two cars during the course of the season, postponing the debut of the new F2005 to the third race, initially expected to be at Imola.

The Ferrari section includes no fewer than 12 cars, of which only seven belong to the new series, while the other chassis were those of the 2004 season that were suitably modified and denoted F2004 M.

Three teams built B versions of their respective cars: the Minardi appeared at Imola, Jordan in France and Toyota with its laboratory car for the penultimate race of the season at Suzuka, a B that foreshadowed the 2006 model. Minardi had started the season with the sterile polemics of Paul Stoddart, which ended in the team fielding one car derived from that of the 2004 season, which had a 2002 chassis no less.

In 2005, the positive 2004 record was repeated: no chassis were destroyed during the year.

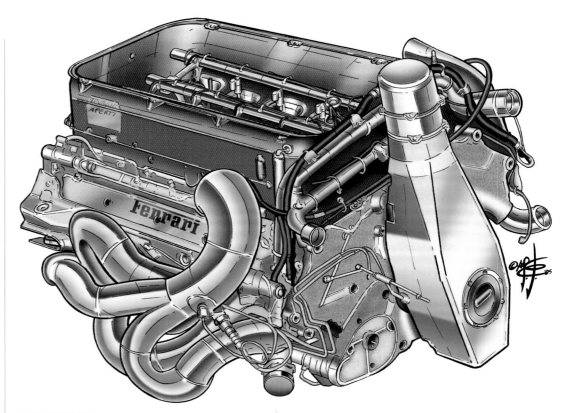

CURIOSITY

The count of the number of chassis built in 2005 sees Toyota in the lead for the second consecutive year with no fewer than 9 compared to the 11 chassis of 2004 and with the last 3 of the series adapted for the new raised front suspension layout.

Then come McLaren and Ferrari with 7 each, even if the latter had fielded 5 F2004 Ms during the early races. They are followed by Williams and Sauber with 6, Red Bull with 5 and Jordan and Minardi with new and 3 old chassis respectively.

The prize for the chassis that won the most in 2005 goes to the 04 McLaren with seven victories scored by Raikkonen, followed by Renault's 04 driven by Alonso; further back is the 07 McLaren of Montoya with two wins, while those with one success were the 03 and 07 of Renault with Fisichella and Alonso respectively, as well as the 245 Ferrari chassis, which took the team's only victory of the season with Michael Schumacher at Indianapolis.

The car with the longest wheelbase was the Jordan at 3,108 mm, followed by BAR and Red Bull with 3,100 mm; the shortest wheelbase was that of the Ferrari at 3,050 mm.

The biggest improvement in quality as far as Constructors' Championship points were concerned was by McLaren at +113 more than in 2004; then came Renault with +87 and Toyota on +57; the biggest loss was registered by Ferrari with 162 points fewer than in 2004; then came BAR at –85 and Williams with –22.

Kimi Raikkonen was dropped back 10 places on the grid three times due to the substitution of the Mercedes-Benz 10-cylinder during practice at Magny Cours, Silverstone and Monza.

FERRARI • F2004M • F2005 • N° 1-2

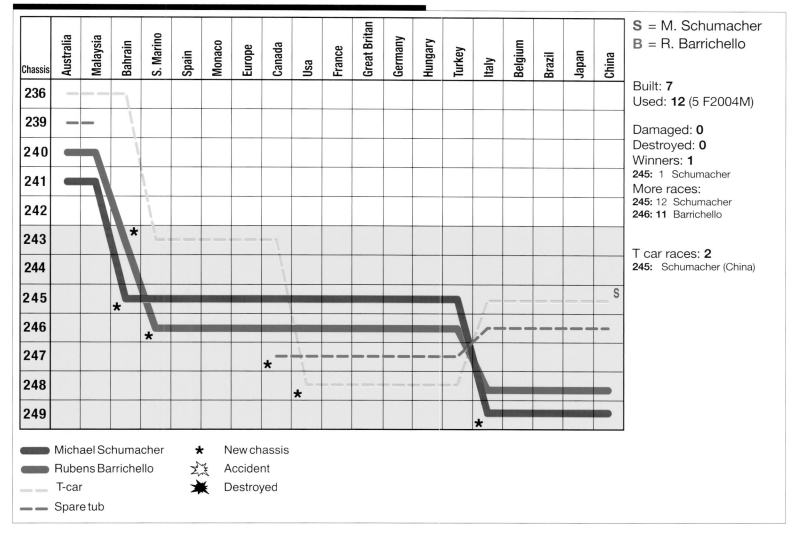

Chassis	Australia	Malaysia	Bahrain	S. Marino	Spain	Monaco	Europe	Canada	Usa	France	Great Britan	Germany	Hungary	Turkey	Italy	Belgium	Brazil	Japan	China
236																			
239																			
240																			
241																			
242																			
243			★																
244																			
245		★																	S
246			★																
247							★												
248								★											
249															★				

S = M. Schumacher
B = R. Barrichello

Built: **7**
Used: **12** (5 F2004M)

Damaged: **0**
Destroyed: **0**
Winners: **1**
245: 1 Schumacher
More races:
245: 12 Schumacher
246: 11 Barrichello

T car races: **2**
245: Schumacher (China)

Legend:
- ▬▬ Michael Schumacher
- ▬▬ Rubens Barrichello
- – – T-car
- ▬ ▬ Spare tub
- ★ New chassis
- ✳ Accident
- ✸ Destroyed

Chassis F2005	243	244	245	246	247	248	249
First run	01-03-2005	24-04-2005	26-03-2005	22-04-2005	19-05-2005	01-11-2005	10-01-2006
Km completed GP	363	0	6.386	5.926	0	2.829	2.363
Km completed Test	21.071	16.245	2.096	0	5.840	2.118	912

McLAREN • MP4 20 • N° 9-10

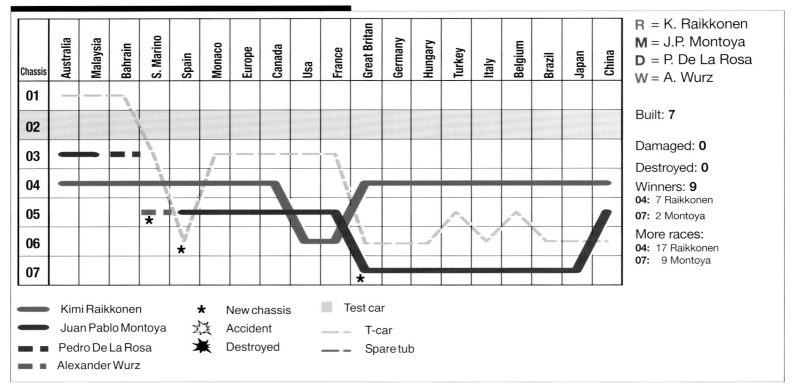

R = K. Raikkonen
M = J.P. Montoya
D = P. De La Rosa
W = A. Wurz

Built: **7**

Damaged: **0**

Destroyed: **0**

Winners: **9**
04: 7 Raikkonen
07: 2 Montoya

More races:
04: 17 Raikkonen
07: 9 Montoya

	Kimi Raikkonen	★	New chassis		Test car
	Juan Pablo Montoya	✶	Accident		T-car
▬ ▬	Pedro De La Rosa	✸	Destroyed	▬ ▬	Spare tub
▬ ▬	Alexander Wurz				

RENAULT • R25 • N° 5-6

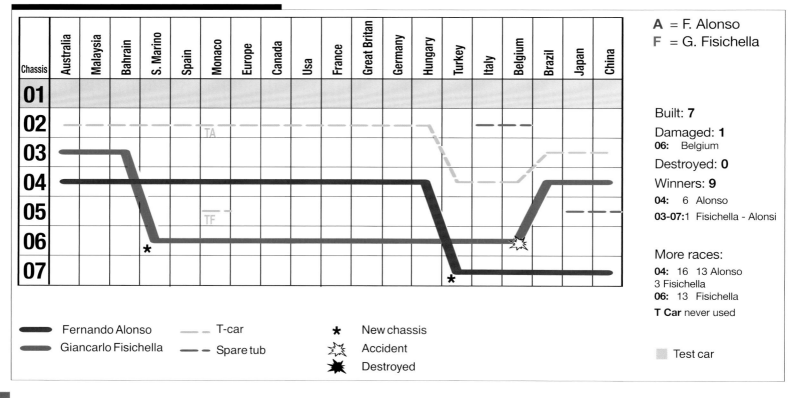

A = F. Alonso
F = G. Fisichella

Built: **7**

Damaged: **1**
06: Belgium

Destroyed: **0**

Winners: **9**
04: 6 Alonso
03-07: 1 Fisichella - Alonsi

More races:
04: 16 13 Alonso
3 Fisichella
06: 13 Fisichella
T Car never used

	Fernando Alonso	─ ─	T-car	★	New chassis
	Giancarlo Fisichella	▬ ▬	Spare tub	✶	Accident
				✸	Destroyed

Test car

TOYOTA • TF105 • N° 16-17

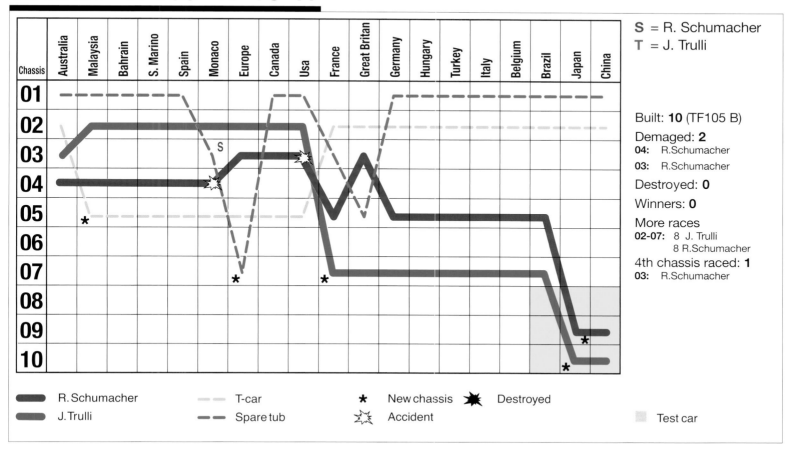

S = R. Schumacher
T = J. Trulli

Built: **10** (TF105 B)
Demaged: **2**
04: R.Schumacher
03: R.Schumacher
Destroyed: **0**
Winners: **0**
More races
02-07: 8 J. Trulli
8 R.Schumacher
4th chassis raced: **1**
03: R.Schumacher

R. Schumacher — — — T-car ✶ New chassis 💥 Destroyed
J. Trulli — — Spare tub 💥 Accident ▨ Test car

	laps completed (%)	finishes	technical failures	accidents	test km	days
Toyota	2113 (95,4 %)	31	2 engine (1)	3	39.274	57
Sauber	2052 (92,7 %)	29	5 hydraulics (1) - engine (1)	2	15.709	35
Renault	1976 (89,3 %)	30	2 engine (1)	4	42.102	52
Ferrari	2131 (88,9 %)	30	4 puncture (2)	4	62.129	132
McLaren	1915 (86,5 %)	27	5 hydraulics (2) - engine (1)	3	35.286	54
BAR	1655 (85,3 %)	19*	7 engine (2) - brakes (3)	1	51.974	56
Jordan	2034 (84,4 %)	32	4 elektrics (2) - hydraulics (2)	2	9.159	21
Williams	1824 (82,4 %)	24	5 engine (2)	7	39.115	58
Red Bull	1708 (77,9 %)	27	3 engine (1)	6	26.988	41
Minardi	1744 (72,4 %)	22	9 gearbox (4)	6	4.013	11

* Disqualified for 2 races

WINNING STRATEGIES

The 2005 season was unique. New rules mean that tyre changing was banned in pit stops. As far as the tyres were concerned, F1 was now endurance racing. It shifted the balance of power in F1, but the rule lasted only one season.

For 2006 the rule was controversially rescinded and tyre changes were reintroduced, so the 19 Grands Prix of the 2005 season stand out as something of an anomaly.

Clearly such a fundamental change had major implications for race strategy. Tactically the benefits of introducing a new set of tyres at a pit stop have always been very important. A new set will offer an immediate injection of pace, typically around 1.5 secs per lap compared the old set, which have suffered degradation over a 20 lap stint. Quite often in modern Grand Prix racing the performance on the first and second laps out of the pits on a new set of tyres has been the decisive factor in winning a race.

On the face of it, then, the immediate reaction of the teams to the banning of tyre changes in 2005 and the accompanying loss of that injection of pace would be 'let's one-stop'. But in practice that was not a viable option because of the risk of the heavy fuel load damaging the tyres in the early stages of the race.

One of the additional rules for 2005 was that a flat spotted tyre could not be replaced, only one which was clearly dangerous and even then there was some doubt, before Kimi Raikkonen's spectacular last lap accident at the Nurburgring, as to what exactly constituted a 'damaged tyre'

The new tyre rules played havoc with race strategies, because the key factor became ensuring that a single set of tyres could perform during the single lap qualifying session on Saturday (and in the early part of the season, Sunday morning as well) and still provide some grip at the end of 70 laps on Sunday afternoon.

As far as the two competing tyre companies were concerned, Michelin were able to marry the two requirements of single lap pace and durability more effectively than Bridgestone. Ferrari were no longer the dominant force.

This was also the final year of single lap qualifying, a format unloved by the spectators, but one which placed a real premium on driver skill. Qualifying with race fuel had become well established and each team had developed its own view on how best to send out the cars for the qualifying lap and the opening phase of the Grand Prix.

Two stop strategies were the norm in 2005 but there were several ways to play it; a standard two stop plan with three roughly equal stints, or a long opening stint followed by two equal shorter stints or a short first stint with the option to three stop or go for two long final stints.

In qualifying, if you were brave, you could make big gains on grid by opting for the latter and running lower fuel loads. Although this meant that your first stint would be short which, according to the computer model, was not the fastest way to do the race, it allowed you to run on a clear track at the front and make the most of phenomenon known as 'field spread'.

Williams' technical director Sam Michael successfully used the short first stint approach at the Nurburgring where Nick Heidfeld scored a memorable second place.

Sam explains 'field spread', "In the opening laps of a GP the field spread is massive. You have the cars leaving the grid in a line, they then cannot follow each other any closer than 1 second apart. With 20 cars that's 20 secs after a lap. You very quickly have a very big spread. If you are in front of that, you have a clear track and can run absolutely flat out, whereas someone 6 or 7 places behind you is

RACE SIMULATOR 2005 CANADA		
Number of laps		70
Total fuel required (kg)		172.75
Target lap time (sec)		75.1
Fuel effect (sec/10kg)		0.255
IF THE START HAD GONE RIGHT	race time for 2 stop strategy (min)	Start
	89.060	0
	Refuelling Amount (kg)	33.0
	Remaining fuel in a car (kg)	
	Estimated lap time (sec)	
	Stationary time (sec)	
	Elapsed time (min)	
IF THE SAFETY CAR WAS NOT DEPLOYED ON LAP 48	race time for 3 stop strategy (min)	Start
	89.058	0
	Refuelling Amount (kg)	33.00
	Remaining fuel in a car (kg)	
	Estimated lap time (sec)	
	Stationary time (sec)	
	Elapsed time (min)	
THE ACTUAL RACE THAT FERRARI AND MSC DID	race time for 3 stop strategy (min)	Start
	89.178	0
	Refuelling Amount (kg)	33.00
	Remaining fuel in a car (kg)	
	Estimated lap time (sec)	
	Stationary time (sec)	
	Elapsed time (min)	

stuck in traffic they cannot make the most of their strategy. There might only be a small amount of difference between your strategy and theirs maybe 3 or 4 secs, but you've won that after a few laps."

But to make the plan work you have to be sure to qualify at the front of the grid and drive the opening stint flat out. There are two significant risks to adopting the short first stint approach; if the driver messes up his qualifying lap, then you are in trouble because you are out of position, stuck in traffic and you lose all the benefit of a light car. The second is if a safety car is deployed before your first pit stop. The field closes up and the opportunity to sprint away at the front is lost. But sometimes even the most compromised situation can still yield a result. Ferrari found themselves in an awkward position at the Canadian Grand Prix where Michael Schumacher used the short first stint approach to qualify on the front row of the grid, but he had a poor start and fell to sixth place on the opening lap.

Unable to make the most of his strategy he was 12 seconds behind the leader when he pitted on lap 12, dropping him to 12th place. Most of the front running cars still had another 12-13 laps of fuel at this point, so it looked very bad for Schumacher. Had things gone right at the start, Ross Brawn would probably have switched him on to a two stop strategy, put in a big fuel load and run two longer final stints to take him to the finish on lap 70, but being so far behind he went for broke on a three stop plan and things conspired in Schumacher's favour after that. First the performance of the Michelins faded, while the Bridgestones held up well, so Schumacher's lap times were competitive as the race unfolded.

Running in clear air he was able to push hard and so by lap 34 he was back up to 6th place. Jarno Trulli in 7th place was far enough behind for Schumacher to be able to pit and retain 6th place. He was now 33 seconds behind the leader and he, like all five cars in front of him, had to pit again.

But then both leading Renaults dropped out; Alonso crashed and Fisichella retired with gearbox problems.

Schumacher was catching third place Jenson Button when the Englishman crashed on lap 47. This brought out the safety car, so Schumacher's deficit of 30 seconds to the leader was wiped out in an instant. Schumacher was able to use the safety car to make his final pit stop and then second place Montoya was black flagged for ignoring the red light at the pit lane exit. Schumacher now found himself in second place, three seconds behind race leader Kimi Raikkonen. And, even more extraordinary, Raikkonen's car had a steering imbalance so he was slower than Schumacher! He fought hard to close the gap to the Finn but couldn't find a way past and so he finished the race just over a second behind.

Having appeared totally out of it on lap 12, Schumacher had ridden his luck and almost won the Canadian Grand Prix.

James Hallen

Fuel comsumption (kg/lap)		2.44	Pit-work efficiency (sec)		2.0		
Tyre degradation (sec/lap)		0.0065	Stationary time		10	Thro(%)	
Fuel load at target lap time (kg)		20.0	Feasible # of laps		29.8	100	
Extra time needed for stop (sec)		12.0	Lap 1 extra time (sec)		6.2		

			1° stop	Out				2°stop	Out					Finish
1	2	11	12	13	14	33	34	35	36	40	41	42	43	70
			70.00								71.46			
28.61	26.17	4.21	1.77	69.33	66.89	20.53	18.09	15.65	13.21	3.45	1.01	70.03	67.588	1.71
81.632	75.257	74.756			76.347	75.315	75.259	75.204	75.148	74.925			76.580	75.076
			9.69								9.85			
		13.862		16.742	18.015	42.023	43.278	44.531	45.784	50.784		53.673	54.950	89.060
			1° stop	Out			2°stop	out			3°stop	Out		Finish
1	2	11	12	13	14	33	34	35	36	56	57	58	59	70
			55.00				55.00				31.46			
28.61	26.17	4.21	1.77	54.33		5.53	3.09	55.65		4.41	1.97	30.99		1.71
81.632	75.257	74.756			75.991	74.932			76.168	75.053			75.688	75.076
			8.04				8.04				5.46			
		13.862		16.708	17.975	41.862		44.714	45.984	71.178		73.981	75.243	89.058
			1° stop	Out			2°stop	out			3°stop	Out		Finish
1	2	11	12	13	14	33	34	35	36	47	48	49	50	70
			55.00				55.00				31.46			
28.61	25.17	4.21	1.77	54.33		5.53	3.09	55.65		26.37	23.93	52.95		1.71
81.632	75.257	74.756			75.991	74.932			76.168	75.555			76.190	75.076
			8.04				8.04				5.46			
		13.862		16.708	17.975	41.862		44.714	45.984	59.887		62.707	63.977	89.178

		5 - 6 **RENAULT**	9 - 10 **McLAREN**	1 - 2 **FERRARI**	16 - 17 **TOYOTA**	7 - 8 **WILLIAMS**
CAR		**R25**	**MP4/20**	**F2004 M - F2005**	**TF 105**	**FW 27**
	Designers	Bob Bell - Rob White Pat Symonds	Adrian Newey Mike Coughlan	Ross Brawn - Rory Byrne Aldo Costa - Paolo Martinelli	Mike Gascoyne Gustav Brunner	Patrick Head - Sam Michael Gavin Fisher - Loic Bigois
	Race engineers	R. Nelson - J. McGill - R. Taffin (5) A. Permane - D. Greenwood - F. Lom (6)	Steve Hallam P. Prew (5) - M. Slade (6)	Chris Dyer (1) Gabriele Delli Colli (2)	Francesco Nenco (17) Ossi Oikarinen (16)	R. Gearing (7) X. Pujolar - T. McCoullough(8)
	Chief mechanic	Jonathan Wheatley	Stephen Giles	Nigel Stepney	Gerard LeCoq	Carl Gaden
CHASSIS	Wheelbase	3139 mm*	3087 mm*	3050 mm	3090 mm	3080 mm*
	Front track	1450 mm	1470 mm*	1470 mm	1425 mm	1450 mm
	Rear track	1420 mm	1405 mm*	1405 mm	1411 mm	1410 mm
	Front suspension	2+1 dampers and torsion bars	2+1 dampers and torsion bars	2+1 dampers and torsion bars	2+1 dampers and torsion bars	2+1 dampers and torsion bars
	Rear suspension	2+1 dampers and torsion bars	2+1 dampers and torsion bars	2+1 dampers and torsion bars	2+1 dampers and torsion bars	2+1 dampers and torsion bars
	Dampers	Penske	McLaren	Sachs (rotary rear dampers)	Sachs - Toyota (rotary rear dampers)	Williams
	Brakes calipers	A+P	A+P	Brembo	Brembo	A+P
	Brakes discs	Hitco	Carbon Industrie	Brembo CCR Carbon Industrie	Hitco	Carbon Industrie
	Wheels	O.Z.	Enkey	BBS	BBS	O.Z.
	Radiators	Marston	Calsonic - IMI	Secan	Nippon - Denso	IMI Marston
	Oil tank	middle position inside fuel tank	middle position inside fuel tank	middle position inside fuel tank	middle position inside fuel tank	middle position inside fuel tank
GEARBOX		Longitudinal Titanium	Longitudinal Carbon	Longitudinal Carbon	Longitudinal Alluminium	Longitudinal Alluminium
	Gear selection	Semiautomatic 6 gears	Semiautomatic 7 gears	Semiautomatic 7 gears	Semiautomatic 7 gears	Semiautomatic 6 gears
	Clutch	A+P	A+P	A+P	A+P	A+P
	Pedals	2	2	2	2	2
ENGINE		Renault RS25	Mercedes FO110R	Ferrari 055	RVX-05	BMW P84/5
	Total capacity	2996.6 cmc*	2996.6 cmc*	2998 cmc	2998 cmc	2998.3 cmc*
	N° cylinders and V	10 - V 72°	10 - V 90°	10 - V 90°	10 - V 90°	10 - V 90°
	Electronics	Magneti Marelli	McLaren el. sys.	Magneti Marelli	Magneti Marellli	BMW Elektronik
	Fuel	Elf	Mobil	Shell	Esso	Petrobras
	Oil	Elf	Mobil	Shell	Esso	Castrol
	Fuel tank capacity	98 kg*	106 kg*	90 kg*	98 kg	90 kg*
	Dashboard	Magneti Marelli	McLaren	Magneti Marelli	Toyota	Williams

CAR TABLE

14 - 15 **RED BULL**	3 - 4 **BAR**	11 - 12 **SAUBER**	18 - 19 **JORDAN**	20 - 21 **MINARDI**
R. B. 1	**007**	**C24**	**EJ 15 - 15B**	**PS04B / PS05**
Mark Smith Guenther Steiner	Geoffrey Willis Gary Savage	Willy Rampf	John Mc Quillium	Gabriele Tredozi
S. Sordo - T. Mayoln (14) R. Hartvelt - A. Damerum (15)	Andrew Shovlin (3) Jock Clear (4)	G. Dall'Ara (11) Mike Krack (12)	B. Joyce (18) P. Bonnington (19)	Andy Thilley R. Adami (20) - L. Mekies (21)
Darren Nichols	Alistair Gibson	Urs Kuratle	Andy Stevenson	Bruno Fanocci
3100 mm	3140 mm	3090 mm	3108 mm	3097 mm
1440 mm*	1460 mm	1460 mm	1445 mm	1480 mm
1410 mm*	1420 mm	1400 mm	1405 mm	1410 mm
2+1 dampers and torsion bars	2+1 dampers and torsion bars	2+1 dampers and torsion bars	2+1 dampers and torsion bars	2+1 dampers and torsion bars
2+1 dampers and springs	2+1 dampers and torsion bars	2+1 dampers and torsion bars	2+1 dampers and springs	2+1 dampers and torsion bars
Koni	Koni	Sachs (rotary rear dampers)	Jordan - Penske	Sachs
A+P	Alcon - Akebono	Brembo	A+P	Brembo
Brembo - Hitco	Brembo	Brembo	Brembo - Carbon Industrie	Hitco - Brembo
O.Z.	BBS	O.Z.	BBS	O.Z.
Marston	IMI Marston - Showa	Calsonic	Secan - Marston	Secan
middle position inside fuel tank	middle position inside fuel tank	middle position inside fuel tank	middle position inside fuel tank	middle position inside fuel tank
Longitudinal Alluminium	Longitudinal Carbon	Longitudinal Titanium	Longitudinal Magnesium	Longitudinal Titanium
Semiautomatic 7 gears	Semiautomatic 7 gears	Semiautomatic 7 gears	Semiautomatic 7 gears	Semiautomatic 6 gears
A+P	Sachs	A+P	A+P	A+P
2/3	2	2	2	2
Ford Cosworth TJ 2005	Honda RA005E	Petronas 05	Toyota TRVX-05	Ford TJ 2005
2998 cmc	2993 cmc*	2998 cmc	2998 cmc	2998 cmc
10 - V 90°	10 - V 90°	10 - V 90°	10 - V 90°	10 - V 90°
P.I.	Honda PGM-F1	Magneti Marelli	Magneti Marelli	Magneti Marelli
BP	Elf	Petronas	Elf	Elf
Castrol	Nisseki	Petronas	Elf	Elf
95 kg	100 kg	98 kg	95 kg*	95 kg
P.I.	BAR	Sauber	P.I.	Magneti Marelli

* extimated value

ENGINES 2005

The most significant new change of the 2005 season on the engine front was the Federation's introduction of the regulation that imposed the use of a single power unit for two races. In an analysis of the championship, therefore, there must be a recapitulation of the use of engines throughout the entire span of 19 Grands Prix. The unit that covered the most kilometres in 2005 was the Toyota RVX-05 number three, used by Tiago Monteiro during the first two weekends in Australia and Malaysia, which clocked up 1,264 km. Just three kilometres less at 1,261 was the Cosworth TJ2005 raced by Friesacher and Doornbos of Minardi in Great Britain and Germany.

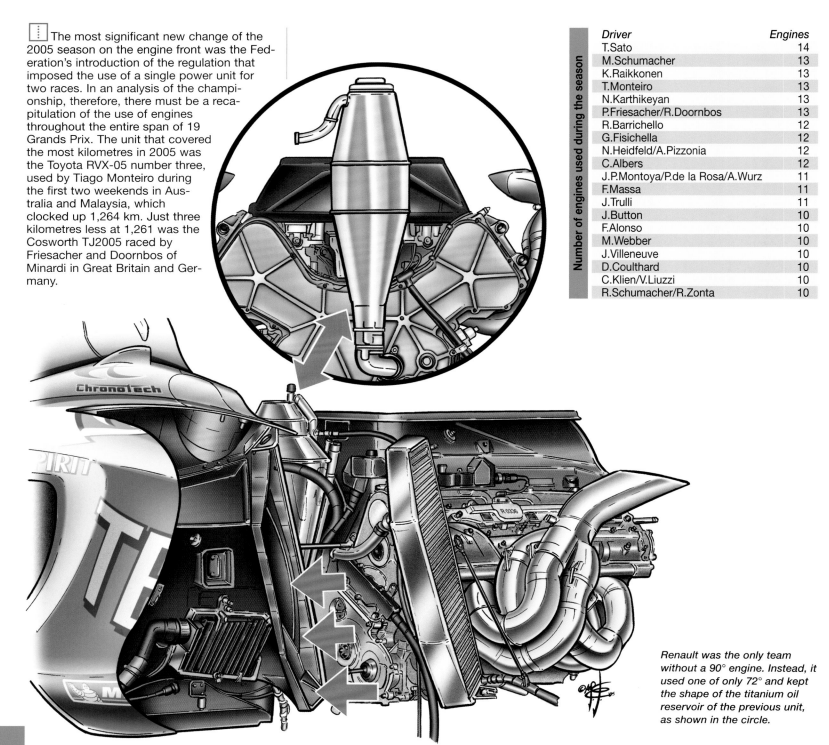

Renault was the only team without a 90° engine. Instead, it used one of only 72° and kept the shape of the titanium oil reservoir of the previous unit, as shown in the circle.

	Driver	Engines
Number of engines used during the season	T.Sato	14
	M.Schumacher	13
	K.Raikkonen	13
	T.Monteiro	13
	N.Karthikeyan	13
	P.Friesacher/R.Doornbos	13
	R.Barrichello	12
	G.Fisichella	12
	N.Heidfeld/A.Pizzonia	12
	C.Albers	12
	J.P.Montoya/P.de la Rosa/A.Wurz	11
	F.Massa	11
	J.Trulli	11
	J.Button	10
	F.Alonso	10
	M.Webber	10
	J.Villeneuve	10
	D.Coulthard	10
	C.Klien/V.Liuzzi	10
	R.Schumacher/R.Zonta	10

	n°	Driver	Unit	km covered	Used in
Engines with the most km	18	T.Monteiro	Toyota RVX-05 (3)	1264	Australia-Malesia
	20	P.Friesacher/R.Doornbos	Cosworth TJ2005 (21)	1261	Great Britain-Germany
	3	J.Button	Honda RA005E (16)	1241	Turkey-Italy
	18	T.Monteiro	Toyota RVX-05 (7)	1235	Bahrain-San Marino
	18	T.Monteiro	Toyota RVX-05 (18)	1229	Europe-Canada
	3	J.Button	Honda RA005E (23)	1225	Japan-China
	19	N.Karthikeyan	Toyota RVX-05 (4)	1225	Australia-Malaysia
	3	J.Button	Honda RA005E (12)	1221	France-Great Britain
	14	D.Coulthard	Cosworth TJ2005 (1)	1214	Australia-Malaysia
	18	T.Monteiro	Toyota RVX-05 (27)	1211	Great Britain-Germany
Engines with the fewest km	19	N.Karthikeyan	Toyota RVX-05 (35)	16	Turkey
	9	K.Raikkonen	Mercedes-Benz FO110R (11)	52	France
	2	R.Barrichello	Ferrari 055 (2)	59	Bahrain
	19	N.Karthikeyan	Toyota RVX-05 (15)	80	Monaco
	18	T.Monteiro	Toyota RVX-05 (25)	87	Great Britain
	6	G.Fisichella	Renault RS25 (18)	90	Belgium
	1	M.Schumacher	Ferrari 055 (22)	119	China
	1	M.Schumacher	Ferrari 053 (1)	174	Australia
	9	K.Raikkonen	Mercedes-Benz FO110R (18)	185	Italy
	8	N.Heidfeld	BMW P84/5 (6)	194	Spain

Monteiro was one of the drivers who exploited his engines the longest: the Portuguese appears in the list of the first 10 engines covering the most kilometres four times.

The engine that travelled the fewest kilometres in 2005 was the Toyota RVX-05 number 35, which was run by Karthikeyan during the Grand Prix of Turkey weekend.
That unit expired after just 16 kilometres or three laps of the Istanbul circuit. In second place is Raikkonen, who ran one of his engines for only 52 kilometres in France, one of the many breakdowns experienced by the Finn during practice, who was forced to occupy awkward positions on the starting grid many times.

Only one engine was fielded during three different weekends in 2005: that was the Toyota RVX-05 number 21, which was used by Jarno Trulli at Indianapolis, Magny-Cours and Silverstone. Although Trulli did not start the American race, that engine still accumulated 1,175 km before being replaced.

Six drivers put in a "perfect" season from the engine point of view, having used only 10 units during the 19 Grands Prix. They were Fernando Alonso (Renault), Mark Webber (Williams/BMW), Jacques Villeneuve (Sauber/Petronas), David Coulthard (Red Bull/Cosworth), Christian Klien/Vitantonio Liuzzi (Red Bull/Cosworth) and Ralf Schumacher, whose Toyota was driven for a few kilometres by Ricardo Zonta during the American weekend. Jenson Button was another who only used 10 engines, but he was subjected to a disqualification and had to sit out the races in Spain and Monaco.

The driver who used the most engines in 2005 was Takuma Sato with 14 in 17 Grands Prix; he was followed by Kimi Raikkonen (McLaren/Mercedes) with 13, Michael Schumacher (Ferrari), Tiago Monteiro and Narain Karthikeyan (both Jordan/Toyota) as well as Patrick Friesacher/Robert Doornbos (Minardi/Cosworth).

Takuma Sato was the leader of the negative list of drivers who covered the lowest average number of kilometres with his engines: his Honda RA005Es ran for an average of just 627 km each, while the drivers with a better yield managed over 900 km for each unit, with an enormous difference in return. The best in this category was Ralf Schumacher, who got an average of 1,004 km from each of his Toyota RVX-05s and was the only driver to exceed 1,000 km.
It is meaningful to note that the drivers who fought it out for the world title are at the other end of this list: Fernando Alonso came third with 998 km per engine and Kimi Raikkonen was the penultimate with 698 km/engine. It is like saying that each of the Alonso engines covered an average of an entire Grand Prix of 300 km more than Raikkonen's.

	Driver	N° engines	km	Average km/engine
Average number of kilometres covered	R.Schumacher/R.Zonta	10	10.047	1004,7
	J.Villeneuve	10	9993	999,3
	F.Alonso	10	9988	998,8
	D.Coulthard	10	9410	941,0
	J.Button	10	9230	923,0
	F.Massa	11	10.101	918,3
	C.Klien/V.Liuzzi	10	9049	904,9
	J.Trulli	11	9791	890,1
	M.Webber	10	8812	881,2
	T.Monteiro	13	11.205	861,9
	R.Barrichello	12	9963	830,3
	C.Albers	12	9855	821,3
	J.P.Montoya/P.de la Rosa/A.Wurz	11	8595	781,4
	G.Fisichella	12	9365	780,4
	N.Karthikeyan	13	9658	742,9
	M.Schumacher	13	9624	740,3
	N.Heidfeld/A.Pizzonia	12	8709	725,8
	P.Friesacher/R.Doornbos	13	9408	723,7
	K.Raikkonen	13	9077	698,2
	T.Sato	14	8784	627,4

Looking at the matter from a strictly engine standpoint, the 2005 season can be summed up with just two numbers: 998 and 698, the average kilometrage covered by the engines of Fernando Alonso and Kimi Raikkonen respectively. It is like saying that, by the end of the championship, the Renault V10s had covered a Grand Prix (300 km) more than the Mercedes-Benz units aboard the McLarens, confirmation that the regulation that imposes the use of a single engine for two racing weekends turned out to be a determining factor in the season's end result. In their last year of life before the introduction of the 2.4-litre V8 for 2006, the V10s were subjected to an especially demanding evolutionary step in an effort to guarantee a distance of the order of 1,000 km without anything breaking at the level of power and usage. That objective was only partially met, because if it is true that just six drivers put together a "perfect" season from the engine point of view – in other words, they used only 10 power units for the 19 Grands Prix – and it is equally true that constructors of great prestige like Ferrari and McLaren undeniably found themselves in difficulty. The disparity of results within the same teams should also be noted, confirmation that the drivers still play a determinate role in achieving reliability objectives, despite the standardisation of the way in which an F1 car is driven, imposed by the ever more invasive electronic regulations. That, for example, was the case with the Honda RA005E, which achieved an optimum km/engine average in Jenson Button's car with 923 km – 10 units for the entire season – but at the same time is in apparent contradiction with the Takuma Sato car, which is in the last place of this particular classification, having only run for a little over 600 km. A difference of the order of 30%, which is far too high to simply be justified by experiments carried out by the Japanese constructor on an engine destined for the team's second driver. The fact of the matter is that, with such ambitious objectives, the procedures and coolness in trying to comply with them become essential, especially when entering and leaving the pits and when refuelling. Rev-

Kimi Raikkonen lost the world championship to Fernando Alonso and his Renault in the main due to the breakdowns of the 10-cylinder Mercedes-Benz power unit, the last to be designed by Mario Illien.

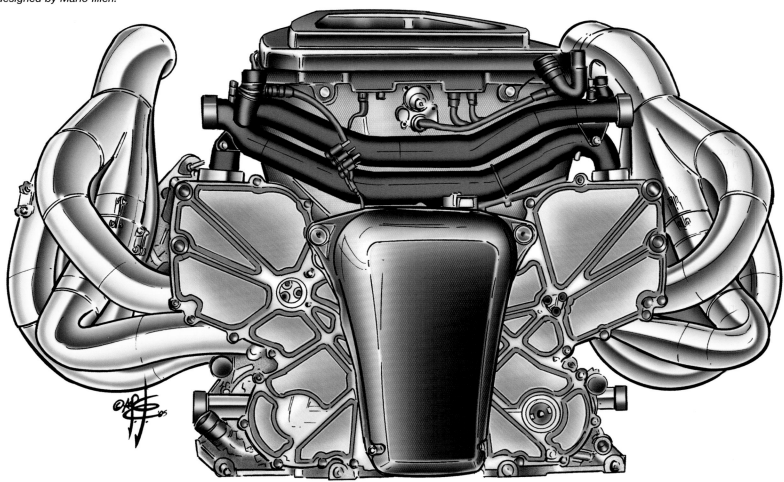

olutions now certified at close to 20,000 rpm constrain designers to their spasmodic use in an effort to keep the drop in mechanical yield under control, determined by friction of operation in constant increase with growing speed, according to an exponential law. For this reason, the water and oil pumps are made to turn at only 30% of the engine's revolutions. But there are also other reasons directly connected with the operation of these components sufficient to inflict such contained limits. The lubrication systems of Formula One engines now all use pumps with lobes, at least for the one that concerns the recovery plant, which has a rapid reduction in efficiency at over 7000 rpm. These are volumetric pumps and take the place of those with gears (which are 'transport' pumps) adopted for the first time on the 1.5-litre V8 Coventry Climax, one of the stars of the championships of the early Sixties. A critical situation aggravated even more by the fact that, in order to further contain the absorption of power, the designers go for an extremely limited pressure of operation, generally ranging between 4 and 5 bar, which falls even further during pit stops to range between 1 and 2 bar. These are values made possible by a circuit that forecasts the introduction of lubricant in an axial sense through a concentric link with the drive shaft, which neutralises the resistance introduced in conventional plants (radial entrance) by centrifugal force. A real challenge to reliability, if one takes into account that, in some cases, the engine and gearbox groups are "served" by a common lubrication plant, despite the different needs of the two groups. And as if that were not enough, with low revs of about 6-7000 rpm typical of a pit stop thrust is relatively modest, operated by combustion gas on the piston crown and compromising the grip of the segments, the functioning of which is assured by none other than combustion pressure, favouring drawing towards the lower part of the engine with the consequent creation of emulsions that can be lethal to the capacity of the engine during the subsequent re-start. It is in this direction that the principal efforts of the designers have been concentrated to guarantee good conditions of survival to the engines also in this delicate phase, using particularly sophisticated degassing systems. It is believed that the Ferrari engine had no fewer than 11 recovery pumps to keep the sump in depression in all circumstances. The optimum value is around 300-400 millibars and the possible passage of this value in a positive field precludes the inevitable breakdown. On the mechanical side, the 2005 engines had a

further increase in bore which, for Ferrari and Honda, exceeded 98 mm and had two objectives: the containment of the piston's average speed and a further lowering of the centre of gravity, today even lower than 180 mm from the ground and where the limit is now only represented by the diameter of the clutch, which is however contained at below three inches, with the operation of the system entrusted to the multiplication of the carbon fibre discs. The high average speed of the piston can, however, determine local overpressure, which has caused breakdowns in some cases and is shown externally by white smoke billowing from the exhausts, unequivocally originating from an incursion into the engine of the cooling liquid, which instantly vaporises in the presence of high temperature. But there is more. If it is true that the power of an engine – at average piston speed parity - is mostly the function of its area ($P = V_{media} \times S$) then it is equally true

In a disappointing season for Ferrari, Maranello's 10-cylinder engine was not without problems, unlike its predecessors. The exhaust system was new and inclined forward due to the car's aerodynamic layout, a deployment also adopted by Sauber.

that the greater surface responds with more difficulty to the stress, also because the primary objective of the designer is to contain the weight of this component, which has now reached almost 230 grams, to limit as much as possible the forces of inertia which, as we shall see later, can have destructive effects. A difficult objective to achieve, because the use of high resistance materials like Berillio have been prohibited by legislation introduced in mid-2002, and magnesium is incompatible with the special benzene additives used in Formula One. Even if when statically analysed, the top of the piston appears completely resistant to deformation, during its operation it conducts itself like the surface of a drum and is subjected to a series of flexing movements that stress it. All of this, added to thermal stress, can lead to the failure - indicated this time by blue smoke from the exhausts, which confirms the entry of lubrication oil into the combustion chamber. As far as the average speed of the piston is concerned, it should be remembered that today's materials enable the attainment of considerable values in the order of 25/26 m/sec, which conforms to maximum speed in correspondence with a rotation angle of 90° of the drive shaft of well over 30 m/sec without particular problems. On the other hand, it is a good idea to remember that in 1992, the 3.5-litre, 12-cylinder Honda RA122/B engine produced an even higher average piston speed. Anyway, it is acceleration that represents the most impervious obstacle to overcome on the road to increasing the rotation revolutions. Acceleration that, applied to the piston mass,

originates forces that can lead to breakage. The Toyota RVX-05 engine is the one that dared most, as it had piston accelerations of the order of 10,000 g which, considering the fact that a piston weighs about 230 grams, determined comparable stress of a couple of tons. Fernando Alonso's world championship owes much to the reliability of the Renault RS25 engine which, however, did not perform as well in Giancarlo Fisichella's car, returning a km/engine average of 781.4 km. Certainly, the French constructor has decided to keep the angle of the cylinder banks at 72°, refusing to fall in line with the now prevailing 90°, more favourable to the lowering of the centre of gravity, the correct disposition of the accessories and the better adjustment of the imperatives dictated by aerodynamics, have weighed in determinant fashion. But it should be remembered it concerns a choice dictated more by the necessity to contain the time of realisation, making reference to previous projects, rather than a purely technical choice. The undeniable advantages in terms of equilibration have, however, played a role that was not marginal in the containment of the terrible vibration that afflicts this typology of engine, but also on the smoothness of power generation, which is then at the basis, in combination with an especially effective electronic control, of the exceptional performance of the Renaults during the start phase. We have already spoken of mechanical yield, but it remains for us to go deeper into the theory of volumetric yield. Ensuring the correct "breathing" of an engine able to turn at 20,000 rpm is an extremely arduous task, at least if one

wants to conserve acceptable intervals of use. In this field, it is BMW who produced the best results with PME values relatively constant in the interval between the maximum rpm torque and that of maximum power. We are talking about 14.5 bar at 16,000 rpm, which corresponds to an engine torque of 39 kg/m. A value that remains consistent until just before 20,000 rpm (about 34 kg/m). A result achieved due to the optimisation of the functional cycle for every single cylinder, also taking into account the specific manner of operation. The biggest obstacle to optimising power is cyclical dispersion. This is a phenomenon for which the method of operation presents an alternation of cycles that are more or less effective. The final power comes from the sum of these values, which assume the characteristics of a magnitude in large part statistical. The objective is, naturally, that of having cycles all aligned with the maximum values, but that is not an easy task. Temperature, pressures and mechanical stress vary from cylinder to cylinder and only from their punctual optimisation by specific phasing of the distribution, ignition and fuel feed obtained in line with auto-adaptive logic is it possible to achieve the maximum overall yield of the engine. The use of the ignition spark plug as a sensor able to take the progress of the pressure in the combustion chamber through analyses of the variation of tension in the electrodes is the optimum solution that enables the provision of all the indications necessary for the achievement of the objective, without the need for invasive sensors that would inevitably compromise the efficien-

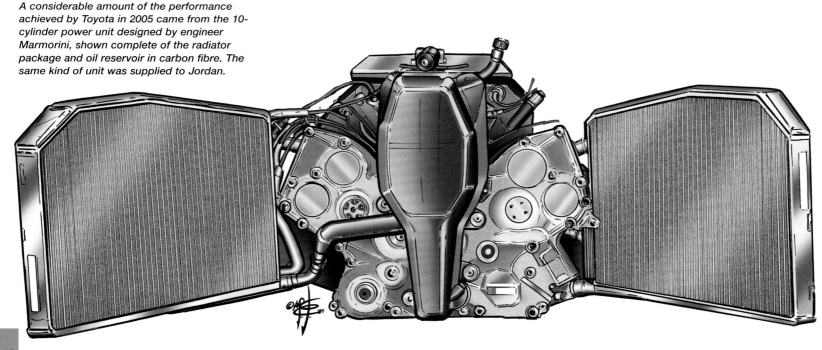

A considerable amount of the performance achieved by Toyota in 2005 came from the 10-cylinder power unit designed by engineer Marmorini, shown complete of the radiator package and oil reservoir in carbon fibre. The same kind of unit was supplied to Jordan.

cy of the combustion chamber. The diminution of the imbalanced pressures between one cylinder and another is also favourably influenced at the mechanical level with little stress on the drive shaft and offers a more ample and sophisticated means of intervening on the antiskid device. An excellent opportunity, given that the anti-spin mechanism is a source of stress that is not marginal as far as the power unit is concerned. Its intervention originates mechanical vibration and determines the unwanted washing of the cylinder with a non-combustible mixture which, gathering in the exhaust, initiates a major increase in temperature that also involves the exhaust and pressure valves. This takes us once again to the evaluation of the importance of the driver in achieving reliability, which also depends on the setting of the anti-spin device that limits its intervention, combining with, rather than substituting, the sensitivity of the driver. At the end of the 10-cylinder engine's long life, it could be interesting to look back at the exceptional progress made during its 17-year career.

Honda were the first to adopt this type of division in 1989. The RA109E was a V10 3.5-litre of 72°. Its maximum power was 660 hp, equal to 188 hp/litre. In 1992, it was Renault's turn with the RS4 which, for the first time, introduced pneumatically operated valves. This was a turning point and the repercussions of the design imposition of the engine were important. Before the introduction of this technique, it was Ferrari's boxer engine that obtained higher revolutions, offering values of more than 14,000 rpm (14,200 rpm), but only at the price of an excessive increase in the load on the springs, with the result that, during a race, the drop in power between the start and finish of a race could exceed 100 CC due to the dramatic stress on the cams. The pneumatically operated valves first used by the French constructor – there is a Honda patent that went back about 10 years, although it was never definitively adopted – enables the achievement of tighter distribution diagrams, so limiting the lift of the valves without conditioning the volumetric yield. Less lift means pistons with "cleaner" crowns, because the slots, which are indispensable in avoiding interference with the valves, can either be reduced or even eliminated. The design is cleaner and also produces advantages, like a more efficient definition of the combustion chamber and the possibility of achieving a higher compression ratio (14:1 and more) despite a continual increase in the bore, permitting the positioning of the grip segment as high as possible. That is how the shielding is reduced by the shell, which inevitably translates into a slower increase in combustion pressure inside the housing of the segment on which depends the grip ability in the final analysis. In combination with

The development for Shell Fuels and Oils for Ferrari 2005

	Fuel	Engine Lube	Gearbox Lube	Performance Benefits
Australia	ULG59L/5	SL-0848	L5361	
Malaysia	ULG59L/5	SL-0848	L5361	
Bahrain	ULG59L/5	SL-0909*	L5361	* Desert Oil - Ultra high protection for Bahrain
San Marino	ULG59L/5	SL-0907	L5361	High efficiency engine lubricant
Spain	ULG59L/7	SL-0907	L5361	
Monaco	ULG60L/2**	SL-0907	L5361	** Desert fuel High temperature performance
Europe	ULG60L/2	SL-0907	L5361	
Canada	ULG60L/2	SL-0907	L5361	
USA	ULG60L/2	SL-0907	L5361	
France	ULG60L/3	SL-0907	L6285	Efficiency upgrade for gear oil, fuel development step
Great Britain	ULG60L/3	SL-0907	L6285	
Germany	ULG60L/3	SL-0907	L6285	
Hungary	ULG60L/3	SL-0907	L6285	
Turkey	ULG60L/3	SL-0907	L6285	
Italy	ULG60L/3	SL-0928***	L6285	*** High protection engine oil for Monza and Belgium
Belgium	ULG60L/3	SL-0928	L6285	
Brazil	ULG60L/3	SL-0907	L6285	
Japan	ULG60L/3	SL-0907	L6285	
China	ULG60L/3	SL-0907	L6285	

pneumatically operated valves, increasingly sophisticated "coating" processes have led to the creation of materials the hardness of which can be assimilated to that of glass, but without producing glass's unwanted fragility, and have facilitated the passage from the direct operation of the cam on the stem of the valve to the one with the interposition of a rocker arm. In this way, the lateral push on the valve stem is neutralised and the diameter of it is contained to just 4.5 mm, favouring extraordinary savings in terms of weight. Just think, the overall valve (in titanium), pneumatic device and rocker arm amount to a weight saving of just over 25% compared to the conventional system.

With the Renault R24 engine, maximum power went up to 760 hp and the specific to 217 hp/litre. With the 3.5 litre, the highest performance for this type of division was achieved in 1994 by Renault, who, with 770 hp, took up position behind the 12-cylinder Ferrari engine, which put out 815 hp. In 2002, after Ayrton Senna's accident at Imola in 1994, cubic capacity was reduced to three litres, but the power output continued to rise: over 880 hp for the BMW unit in the first year of application of the new regulation. In 2003, BMW again led the race for more power with over 910 hp. At mid-season in 2004, Honda's engine had exceeded 930 hp, an output that was also maintained for all of

2005. In 16 years, the specific power of these engines went from the 188 hp/litre of the 1992 Honda unit to over 310 hp/litre of the 2005 Honda, an increase of over 70%, and with revolutions almost doubled, going from 12,800 to 20,000 rpm. And all of this took place while weight was reduced by nearly 50% - engines like BMW with an overall weight of only 83 kg. Exceptional values that have been achieved over the years subjecting the sump, made by inside and outside mechanical casting to the hunt for absolute continuity of thickness. And all of that in the face of a limited distance during an entire Grand Prix, at the end of which no components could be used again –a tendency that was quickly stopped when the regulations brought in at the start of 2005 imposed a longer engine duration.

Mauro Forghieri
Mauro Coppini

NEW REGULATIONS

The Federation introduced a real technical revolution for 2005, intervening on two fronts. Not only did it bring in severe aerodynamic limitations for the cars, the regulations were also significantly modified and that provoked substantial variations in the equilibrium of the world championship. The most important changes concerned the obligation to use a single engine for two races under parc ferme conditions, and the abolition of tyre changes during a race. While ample space is devoted to these aspects in the 2005 engines, brakes and tyres chapters, in this section we shall concentrate in particular on the limitations imposed on aerodynamics, regarded by many technicians as the harshest since 2001, when the height of the front wing from the ground was changed. The areas of intervention affected by the new 2005 norms, which concerned more or less all sectors of the aerodynamic package in order to reduce performance, can be divided into six areas: 1) the front wing; 2) the rear wing; 3) the lateral channels of the diffuser; 4) the elimination of the "seal" at the rear wheels; 5) the reduction of debris on the track; 6) a flexibility test for the rear wing.

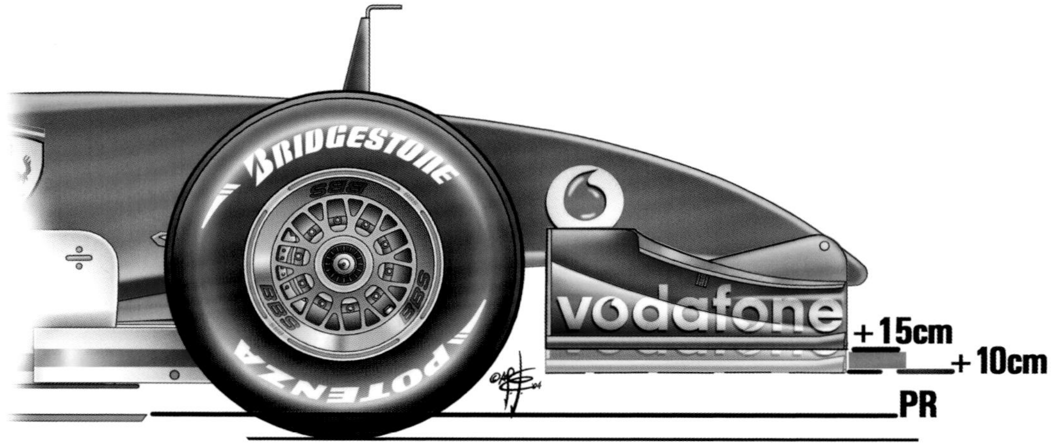

FRONT WING (ART. 3.7.1)

The front wing unit (planes and end plates) was raised another 5 cm in relation to the reference plane, the lowest point on an F1 car, to which all its height measurements refer. Its height has now become +15 cm, +10 cm from 2001 to today.

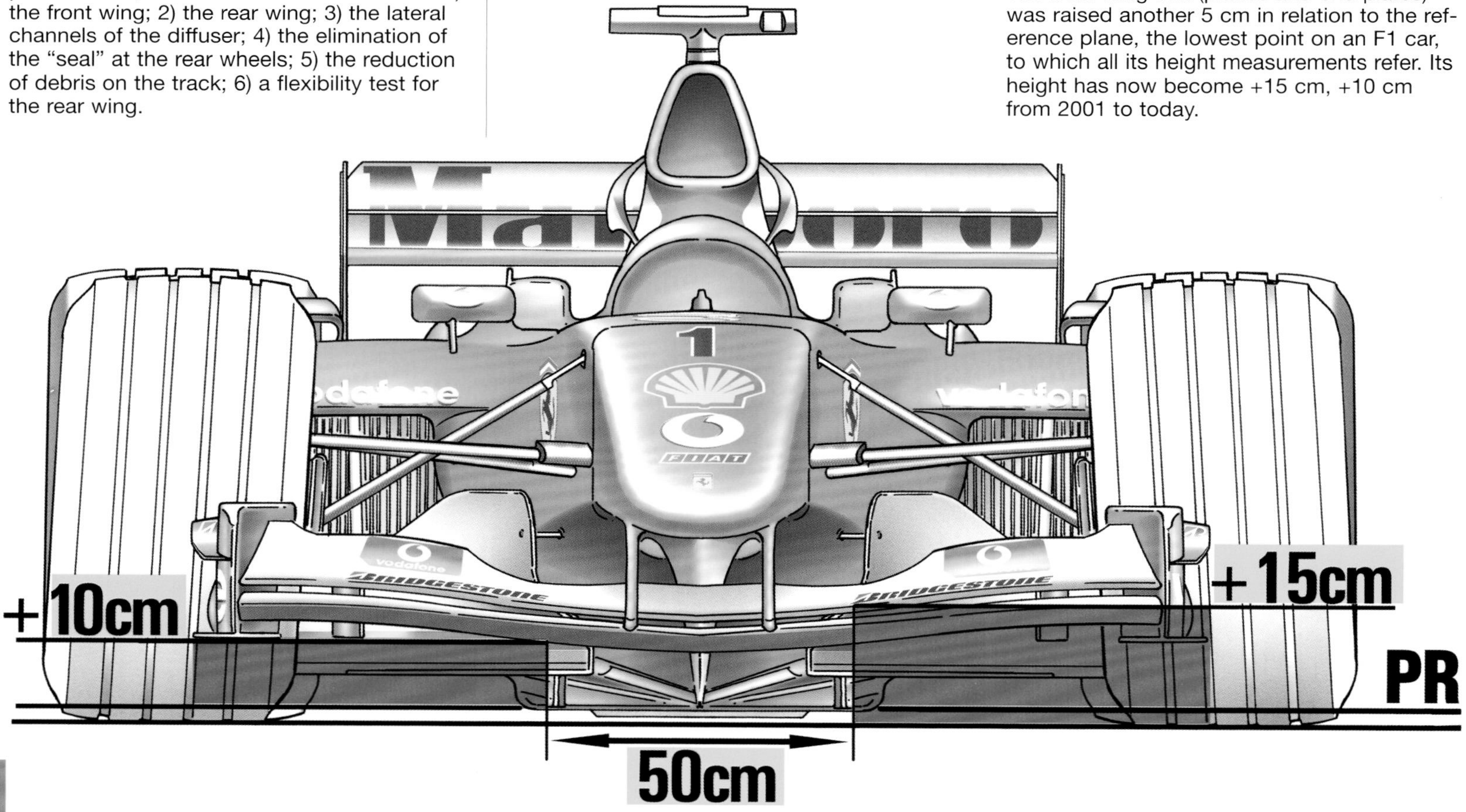

+15cm
+10cm
PR

+10cm
+15cm
PR
50cm

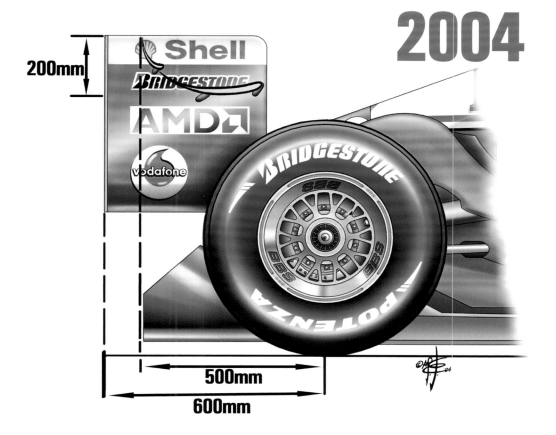

2004

200mm

500mm

600mm

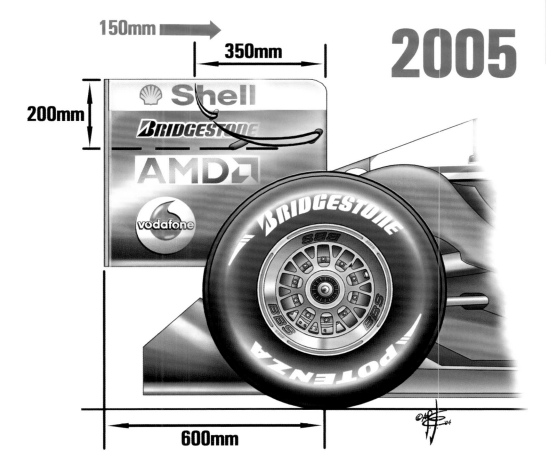

2005

150mm

350mm

200mm

600mm

REAR WING (ART. 3.10.3)

The purpose of the package of aerodynamic restrictions affecting the rear wing overall was to reduce the car's downforce by about 25%. The wing planes were brought forward by 150 mm in relation to the end plates, the overhang of which remained 600 mm. The restriction introduced in 2004 remained in place, calling for only two planes in the upper area and one in the lower. The two planes had to always be in an area 200 mm in height and 350 mm deep: they began at the height of the rear axle with a notable loss of efficiency due to a lesser lever arm force and closer to the car's body; at the same time, they transformed themselves into real travelling advertising panels, given their disproportionate dimensions.

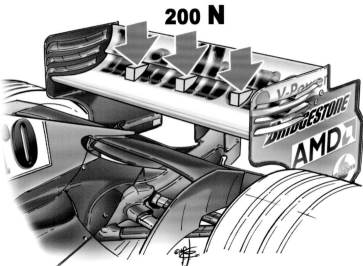

REAR WING FLEXIBILITY TEST (ART. 3.16.6)

At Imola, the Federation made the surprise introduction of a new flexing test for the main plane of the rear wing. Flexing could not exceed 5 mm when a load of 200 N was applied in three precise points of the wing: in the centre, 250 mm from the longitudinal axis of the car, in practice midway between the centre and the wing's end plate. Teams had to supply a small template 50 mm wide that reproduced the shape of the plane so that this verification could be carried out, stopping itself no more than 10 mm from the trailing edge.

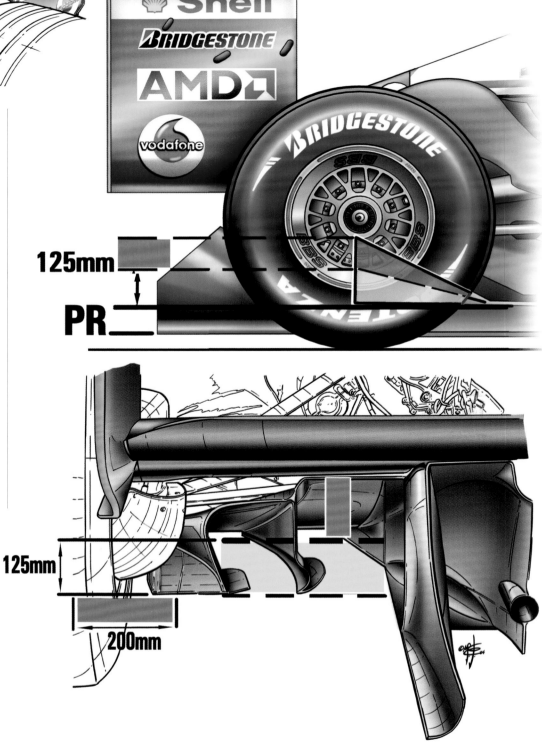

LATERAL CHANNELS OF THE DIFFUSER (ART. 3.12.7)

Another limitation concerned the lateral channels of the diffuser, the progressive height development of which was previously to have been considered without limitation. Now, only the central channel was restriction free. The height of the lateral channels was fixed at a maximum limit of 125 mm, resulting in a sharp fall in the efficiency of the diffusers, a drop recorded on laboratory cars at between 8% and 10%, which also meant less seal created with the rear wheel, due to the introduction of a "hole" around the rear tyres.

ELIMINATION OF THE REAR WHEEL "SEAL" (ART. 3.8.4)

The 2005 limitations imposed by the Federation also included the elimination of the "seal" between the car's lower body and the rear wheels. The loss measured by the laboratory car was of the order of 5%, also because in recent years the teams had taken particular care with this seal, which delivered greater efficiency in the area of the rear diffuser channels. That zone now had to include a "hole", the perimeter of which was situated at 400 mm from the rear axle – the tyres have a radius of 300 mm – and 200 mm towards the internal part of the car. In that way, a rectangle was created that left an empty space of around 100 mm and could have a connecting radius between the two sides of 140 mm.

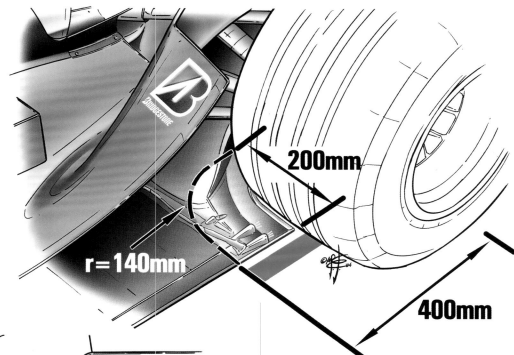

REDUCTION OF DEBRIS ON THE TRACK (ART. 3.4.3)

To reduce the risk of punctures caused by composite material debris on the track after an accident, as happened in the past at Indianapolis, Budapest and Spa, the Federation obliged the teams to fit a Kevlar skin to all the aerodynamic elements that could be easily broken off, like the front wings, front and rear end plates and the barge boards behind the front wheels. The illustration shows the inside of the Renault's end plate in which the application of the Kevlar skin can be seen.

NEW SOLUTIONS

As often happens in years of great technical upheaval, many new developments appeared in 2005, especially in the first few races. Most of them were aimed at recovering downforce and for that reason they are illustrated in the Aerodynamics chapter. As the season continued, a number of tendencies that had emerged
in 2004 were consolidated in 2005, a year in which they became even more important due to further limitations as a result of the new regulations concerning the cars respective sectors of development. The two most important teams dictated the law as far as new tendencies were concerned: Renault and McLaren, with the introduction of features that had already made their appearance in 2005 but which will certainly be the subject of further development the following year. The first concerned the abandonment of both the double and single keels in favour of a middle-of-the-road solution that was completely new for the cars with noses raised from the ground, like those of the current Formula One.

GOODBYE KEELS

Strangely, Renault and McLaren were the only teams to have dropped both the double and single keels, replaced by extremely innovative wishbone suspension mounts. The R25 had a new V-shaped tubular structure that generated the same structural advantages of the central bulb to which others of an aerodynamic character were added that were linked to a

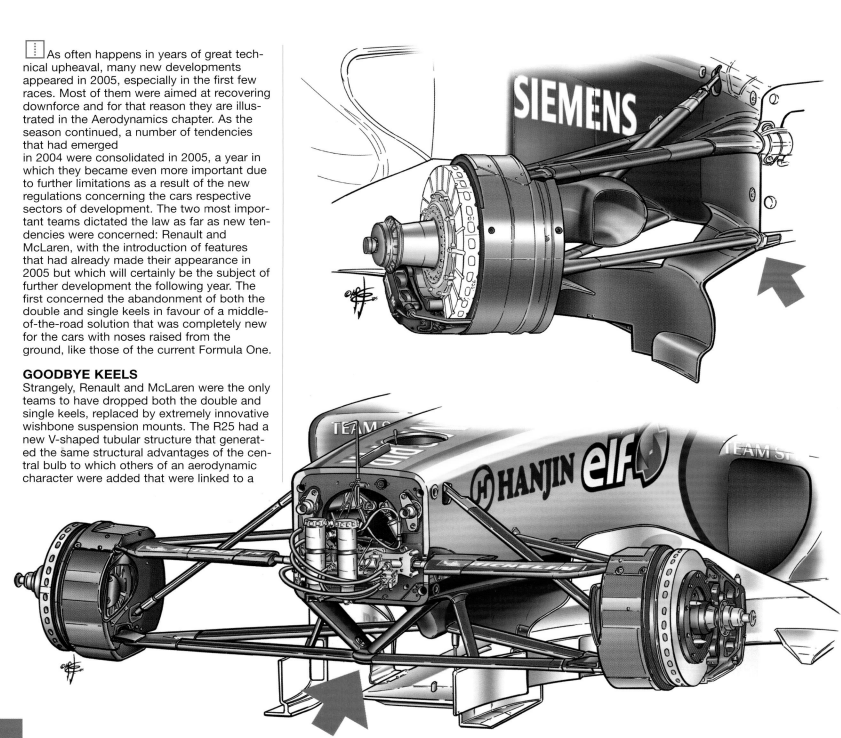

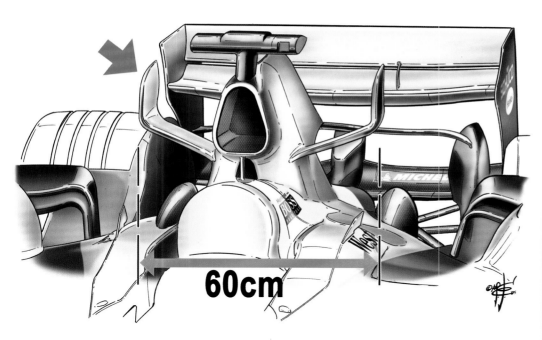

60cm

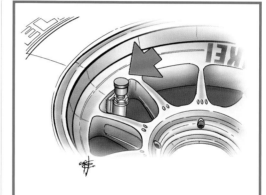

better quality of airflow in that area, which is especially critical to the lower aerodynamics of the car. This is a feature considered by Pat Symmonds as the star development of the French car. After two seasons in which it remained faithful to the twin keel, McLaren's MP4-20 practically went back to using the split lateral mounts in the low area of the chassis, as was the case with the cars that preceded the great innovation by Jean Claude Migeot on the 1990 Tyrrell 019. It will be interesting to see who between Renault and McLaren makes more converts among the 2006 cars, which will most probably not have central keels any more.

Toyota was quicker than all the other teams by fielding their laboratory car for the last two races of 2005: the car, which foreshadowed the future TF106, was inspired by the MP4-20. The illustration shows how all the suspension (on the right) was designed in the B version to be able to eliminate the central keel mount.

THE McLAREN "HORNS"

Without doubt, the prize for the most unusual aerodynamic feature should go to McLaren for the "Viking horns" behind the engine air intake of the MP4-20, a feature that stayed on the cars throughout the season except at Monza: its purpose was to better equilibrate the car's aerodynamic load. It did so in two ways: by cleaning and channelling the air flow towards the rear wing and by guaranteeing a minimum input of vertical load into the area close to the car's centre of gravity.

VARIATION OF TYRE PRESSURE

From the opening race in Australia, four teams – Ferrari, Williams, McLaren and Renault – brought in a further sophistication that enabled them to vary their cars' tyre pressures during pit stops in order to optimise the management of the covers over the entire race span. As early as the 2002 season, McLaren had been monitoring and checking tyre pressure during the race by telemetry, which was copied in 2004 by Ferrari and Williams. Now, they have moved on to the active phase by intervening to change the pressures and preserve their tyres from a distance. Ferrari and Renault had added to the large valve that recorded the pressure another more robust one of almost double the diameter of the traditional valve for their tyres' inflation fitted with a blocking nut. Williams used this large valve without protection, while at McLaren the same valve joined another two and had a plastic cap, a feature that was not used much during the season.

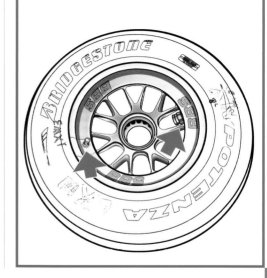

CENTRAL EXHAUSTS

Ferrari must be credited with introducing a further sophistication in the installation of an engine in a car even if Sauber, who used the same power units, beat Maranello by making its track debut with its exhausts farther forward. A feature linked to greater aerodynamic exploitation of the bulk of the exhausts, which, positioned in that way, enabled the narrowing of the so-called Coke bottle zone at the back of the car by about 20-30 cm. Paradoxically, the less bulk in height of the lateral channels of the diffuser imposed by the regulations opened new frontiers of development in thermal dissipation from the sidepods, reducing the blocking effect when exiting the highest lateral channels. From this came the idea to take to the extreme the concept of mounting the exhaust manifold practically upside down unifying the terminal as much as possible at the centre of the car.

The illustration in yellow shows the new exhausts design and compare them with those of 2004. Note that the F2005 had inclined V-mounted radiators like those of the 2004 Sauber.

SAUBER EXHAUSTS

A comparison between the Ferrari layout of the new upside down exhausts located farther forward, which were given their debut by Sauber. They had been brought forward about 20-30 cm, were extremely low and more unified to the engine. Note the sophisticated split radiator layout, angled between each other.

TOYOTA BRAKE INTAKES

Toyota came out with the most extreme version of the new tendency to completely fair the rear brake discs during the last few races (they are illustrated in the Brakes and Tyres chapter) to avoid the heat, directed vertically towards the internal walls of the rims, to interfere with the temperature and, secondly, with tyre pressures. The expelled hot air was directed to the outer central zone of the rim in an area that could also be exploited from the aerodynamic point of view.

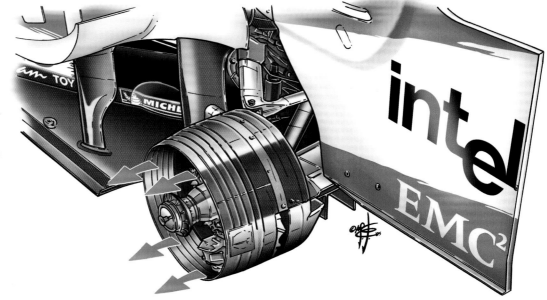

TALKING ABOUT TYRES AND BRAKES

The banning of tyre changes during the races for 2005 posed a harsh new challenge for teams and tyre manufacturers alike. In concert with new aerodynamic restrictions, the 'endurance' tyres contributed to a slight increase in lap times. Despite the new regs, both Michelin and Bridgestone began with further evolutions of their respective designs, tailored to meet the new demands. But Michelin development – particularly with regard to rear constructions - picked up massively in the second half of the year, triggered by a catastrophic weekend for them at Indianapolis.

Overall, it appeared as if the Michelin family of tyre responded better to the challenge of the new regulations than the rival Bridgestone which won only once – and that at a race in which the Michelin cars did not take part, the US Grand Prix.

The fiasco at this race was the dominant tyre-related issue of the year and triggered by the inability of the Michelin tyre to withstand the loads imposed upon it through Indianapolis' banked turn 13. The Toyotas of Ricardo Zonta and Ralf Schumacher were the first to reveal this problem in the Friday practice sessions. Both suffered casing failures of the left-rear, with Schumacher suffering a heavy impact with the turn 13 wall that briefly hospitalised him. Subsequent investigation of other Michelin cars revealed signs of imminent similar failures. Michelin advised its teams that it could not guarantee the safety of the tyre for more than 10 laps – and this ultimately led to the race being held with only the six Bridgestone-shod cars.

The combination of vertical and lateral loads imposed upon a tyre through turn 13 is unique within the F1 calendar. The vertical load is in the order of 800kg per tyre for 5-6 seconds. But this is only an average. In 2005 the *peak* loads were found to be as high as 1200kg – well beyond previous years. The 2005 generation of cars, relying more on the upper surface for their aerodynamic performance than under the old regulations, tended to generate greater peak tyre loads because their aero performance was not as consistent as before. Previously, when more

of the aerodynamic load was derived from ground effect from the lower front wing endplates and a higher-performance diffuser at the rear, the total aero load at any given moment was less sensitive to variations in pressure or turbulence. With the regulation increased height of the endplates and restriction on diffuser dimensions for 2006, the less consistent aero loadings created more aerodynamic 'bouncing' – which the tyre had to absorb. This is essentially why the peak tyre loadings through the turn were much higher than before.

Moreover, the lateral load through turn 13 is not of the conventional type either – because of the angle of the track surface. In a conventional non-banked corner the inner shoulder takes much of the lateral load. On a banked corner however, there is a big input force also

to the outside shoulder. This combination of forces places big demands upon a tyre's construction. The Michelin, with its flexible sidewalls and heavily steel-bolstered belt was particularly susceptible in as much as the flexing sidewalls allowed the steel belt to move within the casing, which ultimately collapsed.

Teams could offset the loads to the outer shoulder on the banking by running some negative camber in the rear wheels. But with a following straight where the cars run at around 200mph for up to 17s, negative camber heats up the inner shoulder excessively, increasing the risk of a high speed blow-out going into turn one.

Indianapolis aside, Michelin enjoyed their most dominant season to date. Their pure

BRIDGESTONE

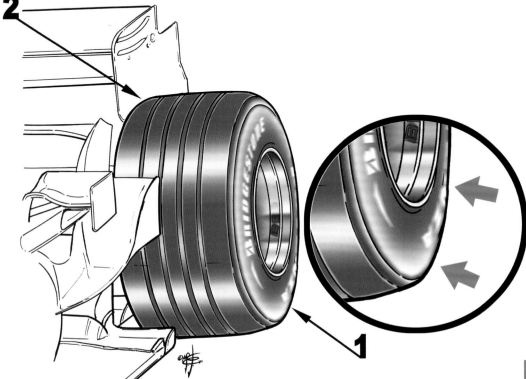

radial construction was extremely well suited to the new emphasis on low wear rates. The plies that comprise the belt of the tyre run at or close to 90-deg to each other. The circumferential plies keep the tyre from expanding and contracting as it is accelerated and braked. They largely determine the tyre's springing, braking and traction. The plies running radially across the tyre give stability and directional response. With a pure radial, these two sets of plies do completely separate tasks, with no overlap. The belt is reinforced by steel, enabling tread and sidewall to be completely separated.

The stiffly bolstered tread area meant the Michelin tread moved less as it came into its contact patch. Furthermore, that contact patch itself was allowed to stay more planted to its path as the sidewalls flexed to accommodate the loads. All this helped the Michelin tread run cooler than that of the Bridgestone – for a comparable compound softness anyway.

To keep the rear tyres in the ideal operating band of 90-100deg C and away from a blistering threshold of around 140deg C, the Bridgestone tended to need a harder, less grippy compound than the Michelin. Compared to the Bridgestone, the French tyre was able to utilise compounds with a higher hysteresis - ie with rubber capable of absorbing more energy, which drapes itself more fully over the track surface, but which generates more heat as a result – for a given tread temperature.

Tyre wear increases dramatically as the tread temperature goes up – and the Bridgestone's wear rates over the years have usually been higher than the Michelin's. This didn't much matter when a set of tyres had to last only for one stint of 15-20 laps and when Bridgestone could enjoy competitive grip without being too concerned about wear rates. But it mattered a lot when they were required to endure a full distance. Effectively, the new regulations drastically narrowed the choice of feasible compounds for Bridgestone because of the greater propensity to run hot imposed by the construction. By contrast, Michelin were barely affected.

The basic grip of a compound is determined by its hysteresis – its ability to absorb the energy put into it. The rubber and other chemical constituents form a compound that is visco-elastic – ie with a deformability somewhere between that of a liquid and a solid. The more towards a liquid a compound is, the 'softer' it is said to be. A softer compound will tend to have a higher hysteresis – but not necessarily so, depending upon its precise chemical make up.

The rate at which a compound responds to an increase in load is not consistent. There is a delay in how it reacts to the loads – because of the elasticity of the material. So if the frequency of the loads is too high, preventing the compound from returning to a state of equilibrium between the loads, it stiffens, won't absorb as much energy and loses some of its grippiness. In this way, the compound is effectively harder at high frequency input loads and softer at lower ones.

Running too cool will have the same effect. There is an inverse relationship in the effect on a compound's softness between the frequencies of the loads and the compound temperature. To give an approximate feel for this relationship, at low frequencies (say between 10 and 105 Hz) an increase in frequency by a factor of 10 hardens the compound by about as much as a temperature drop of 7-8 deg C from the ideal.

The higher the hysteresis, the more heat will be generated (because it is absorbing more energy). The ideal running temperature of the tread – where the hysteresis of the compound will be at its maximum – is just above that at which the compound hardens, ie somewhere between 90-100deg C. So the restriction upon how soft you can go with the compound is determined by how much heat it will generate. This will of course vary between circuits, weather conditions, cars and set ups – and constructions. The Michelin construction generally allowed for a softer compound than did the Bridgestone. It may also be that the Michelin compounds allowed for a greater degree of hysteresis for a given softness. It's still suspected that the French company has a better range of polymers, allowing for longer molecular bonds to form during the vulcanisation process (where the addition of sulphur creates bonds between the various molecules of chemicals).

The 'base' softeness/hardness of the compound - before the effects of load frequencies and excessively cool temperature are considered – is referred to as its modulus, where low-modulus = soft and high-modulus = hard. A low-modulus compound will generate more 'chemical' grip, whereby the rubber of the

contact patch chemically bonds with the surface of the track. It will also generate more 'mechanical' grip, whereby the unsymmetrical way the rubber drapes itself over the rough points of the surface (because of its hysteresis) creates a delayed reaction that tries to pull the rubber back to equilibrium. This force is pulling in the opposite direction to that imposed by the cornering loads and thereby increases grip. Chemical grip generally occurs between frequencies of 106-109 Hz. Mechanical grip predominates between 102-106 Hz.

When the circuit layout imposed only low wear rates on the tyres and Bridgestone were therefore not so badly compromised in how soft they could go on compounds, they appeared fully competitive. In these circumstances the Bridgestone appears to have stronger mechanical grip than the Michelin (possibly because its stiff sidewalls pull the tread rubber back to equilibrium with more force). This is also a likely contributor to the Bridgestone wet weather tyre traditionally being quicker than the Michelin equivalent in heavy rain (as in Suzuka Saturday morning practice when Schumacher's Ferrari was fastest by over 2s, with Narain Karthikeyan's Bridgestone-shod Jordan second fastest). In heavy rain mechanical grip is the dominant factor as the chemical bonding process breaks down. The downside for Bridgestone is that when the surface is merely damp it cannot generate enough heat to give maximum hysteresis and so its compound is artificially hard. By contrast the Michelin can use its better chemical bonding to generate the heat necessary to get the mechanical process working.

On the low-wear track of Melbourne for the season opener, Bridgestone appeared fully competitive. But in the high-wear, hot races of both Malaysia and Bahrain, they ran as soft a compound as they dared in an effort to help Ferrari compete with the dominant Renaults but found that their wear rates were alarmingly high. Rubens Barrichello had to retire in the former race as his rear tyres were down to the casing. They were in a similar condition when he completed the distance in Bahrain. Thereafter Bridgestone were forced to adopt a more conservative compound policy as the limitations imposed by the regs on their particular philosophy of construction became more apparent. Only at other low wear tracks, such as Imola, Montreal and Indianapolis were the Bridgestones competitive.

The Bridgestone remained more of a crossply/radial amalgam. They tend to run their circumferential plies at a slight angle, overlapping their role slightly with the radial plies. In theory it makes for enhanced lateral performance. The tread and sidewall are less rigidly separated, requiring less bolstering of the tread but strong sidewalls without much flexibility. It was these very stiff sidewalls that allowed Bridgestone to suffer no problems at all through Indianapolis' turn 13 but which also limited performance on high-wear tracks. The stiff sidewalls effectively transfer more of the forces onto the tread than the flexible Michelin sidewalls, thereby making the tread run hotter, thereby forcing harder compounds in order to keep wear in check.

For 2005 Bridgestone concentrated on a variation of the rear construction they had introduced at Hungary in 2004. This was a move towards a more Michelin-type of philosophy, but only a small one. The aim was to limit the distortion of the tread as it entered its contact patch, in order to improve the heat durability. A squarer, more rigid, (more Michelin-like) crown was the visible manifestation of this aim. At the same time the very rigid sidewalls were allowed a little more flexibility. In 2004 this type of construction had proved fast but the construction itself was not durable. For 2005 the aim was to improve the durability of the construction without losing its performance. Further bolstering of the tread area and a further softening of the sidewalls saw this aim achieved in the December of the off-season.

Only then did Bridgestone feel able to begin looking at compound developments. In this they were less successful. No real compounding progress was made and for most of the season Bridgestone/Ferrari were mired in a narrow band of available options.
A front construction was tried using a similar tread movement-limiting philosophy to the rear but it was not successful, given that as a steered tyre it depended upon a certain amount of tread movement to generate the camber thrust that helped its initial turn in. As the limitation was in rear tyre performance, so development was thereafter concentrated on that and the front construction design remained static.

Sometimes the problem was manifest in the front tyres – particularly during qualifying – in that they were not getting up to temperature quickly enough. When Felipe Massa tested the Bridgestone-shod Ferrari prior to Monza after a season with the Michelin-shod Sauber, he felt a lack of front-end grip. But that was a symptom rather than a cause.
The regulations that stipulate the same compound for all four tyres ensured that the fronts were usually of harder compounds than they could have used because the rear tyre's deficiencies imposed a limit on compound softness.

At Magny Cours mid-season, after extensive analysis of various track surfaces, came a new Bridgestone compound designed to generate more chemical grip. It succeeded in giving a tyre that got quickly up to temperature and which therefore could qualify reasonably well, but it did not retain its performance well as the race unfolded. On the more abrasive and faster circuit of Silverstone it was even less suitable and was used thereafter only at Turkey. At Hockenheim Michael Schumacher debuted a third Bridgestone compound family. It gave enhanced grip but its wear rate was high, a pattern that was repeated in Hungary where Schumacher set pole but finished second. At the end of the year a new construction based on the '06 tyre was tested but not raced.

Up until Indianapolis Michelin used front and rear constructions lightly developed from 2004, with some new compounds. The F20 was a development of the previous year's F15 and used by pretty much all the Michelin teams except Renault who usually stayed with the less grippy F19. This was for reasons of car balance. With the heavier rearward weight bias of their car, Renault found the grip of the F20 tended to upset the rear end. For the first few races the standard Michelin rear casing was the R14, upgraded to the stronger R15 at Barcelona. It was this that proved unsuitable at Indy.

Thereafter Michelin rear construction improved at a huge rate as the advanced research team sought to understand the problems at Indy. Michelin estimate that they made more development in this area between mid season '05 and the equivalent period in '06 than they had done in the four and a half seasons prior to that. Circuit-specific constructions replaced the previous global solutions, and for the high-speed direction changes of Spa and Suzuka the R18 was introduced. This abandoned the previous asymmetrical sidewall (softer outer shoulder, stiffer inner) that had been introduced to improve direction change and which may have contributed to the problem at Indy. But for the slower tracks the older design was retained, albeit with circuit-specific tweaks.

Tyre performance again dominated the performance pattern of the season, with the proviso that although Bridgestone did not seem to adapt as well to the new regulations as Michelin, their problems were exacerbated by a Ferrari with aerodynamic shortcomings when compared to the cutting edge designs of the Michelin-shod Renault and McLaren.

Mark Hughes

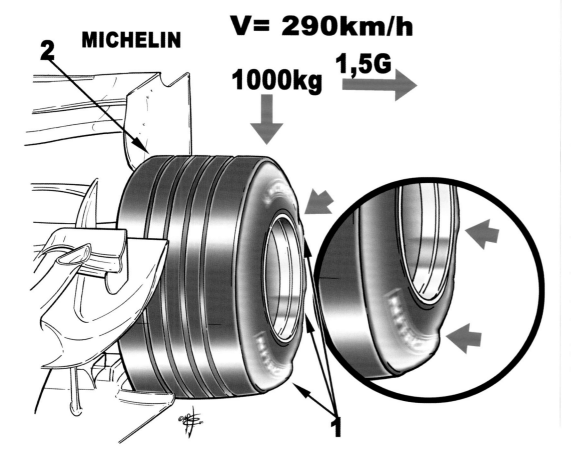

BRIDGESTONE

Australia

	Ferrari	Jordan	Minardi		Williams
HARD	MSC			HARD	
SOFT	RB	NK & TM	CA & PF	SOFT	MW & N...

There were 5 compounds available from Bridgestone. Michael Schumacher was 4th with a harder Prime tyre and Rubens Barrichello was 9th using the softer rubber. Barrichello went for grip and Michael went for car balance. Jordan and Minardi opted to use the Soft which was one step softer than the one Barrichello used. Both tyres performed well for Ferrari as there was not much difference in lap time. However, Hirohide Hamashima (Head of Tyre Development, Bridgestone Motorsport) indicated that they should have brought softer compounds for the Italian team. As far as wet tyres were concerned, the extreme wet performed well since Bridgestone runners dominated the Saturday morning sessions that were wet.

Malaysia

	Ferrari	Jordan	Minardi		Williams
HARD	MSC	NK & TM	CA & PF	HARD	
SOFT	RB			SOFT	MW & N...

Bridgestone took only 3 specifications of tyres from their medium range. Hirohide Hamashima (Head of Tyre Development, Bridgestone Motorsport) described the soft compounds as 'a bit adventurous' but again they lacked qualifying speed. The Bridgestones took some time to get up to the optimum temperature but they lacked pure grip. Rubens Barrichello and Michael Schumacher chose different tyres but that did not make much difference. They were more than 1 sec. adrift of Alonso in the first qualifying session and eventually they could only manage to get 12th and 13th position on the grid. Bridgestone predicted that the race could be a different story but it was not the case. It should be noted that Bridgestone brought new extreme wet-weather tyres after testing them in Valencia.

Bahrain

	Ferrari	Jordan	Minardi		Williams
HARD				HARD	
SOFT	MSC & RB	NK & TM	CA & PF	SOFT	MW & N...

There were 4 compounds from the medium range and 2 different front tyre constructions available from Bridgestone and this led to a total of 4 different specifications of tyres. The new front tyre constructions increased the contact patch and Ferrari, who rushed to introduce the new F2005 car in Bahrain, chose to run this with the soft compound. Jordan also decided to run the soft compound that was believed to be the same as the one they used in Malaysia but with the older front tyre construction. Michael Schumacher grabbed second place on the grid and chased the leader Alonso in the race. Barrichello, who could not do much running on Saturday morning due to a problem, was forced to use Michael Schumacher's set-up and he struggled with excessive wear on his rear tyres in the final laps of the race.

San Marino

	Ferrari	Jordan	Minardi		Williams
HARD		NK & TM	?	HARD	
SOFT	MSC & RB		?	SOFT	MW & N...

Bridgestone tested more than 20 specifications of tyres with Ferrari during a three week break between the Bahrain GP and the San Marino GP. They brought 5 specifications with new rear construction. The concept behind this construction change was to help reduce degradation on the rear tyres. This showed significant improvement in tyre consistency. Because of an error he made in the 2nd qualifying session, Michael Schumacher started from 12th on the grid but he put in a storming drive to move up the second in the race.

Spain

	Ferrari	Jordan	Minardi		Williams
HARD	MSC & RB	NK & TM	CA & PF	Option	
SOFT				Prime	MW & N...

Circuit de Catalunya was resurfaced during the winter break and became easier on tyres but Bridgestone chose tyres from their medium to hard range. Prior to the Spanish GP, Bridgestone and its partner teams tested up to 15 specifications of tyre in Mugello (with Ferrari and Minardi) and Silverstone (with Jordan). There were 4 different compounds to choose from. Ferrari chose their tyres with new front tyre construction to go with new rear tyre construction that was introduced in Imola. However, partly due to this new construction change, Ferrari struggled and could not find car balance in the practice sessions. Ferrari continue to struggle during the race and Michael Schumacher suffered two consecutive punctures - first on the left rear tyre, then the front left tyre. The cause of those two punctures was not identical. It was believed that Bridgestone traced the left rear problem to the fact that the tyre pressure fell below its proper figure at the time of safety car period and the tyre suffered a high degree of deformation that eventually destroyed its construction. On the other hand, the left front tyre was damaged by picking up some debris.

Monaco

	Ferrari	Jordan	Minardi		Williams
Prime	MSC & RB	NK & TM		HARD	MW & N...
Option			CA & PF	SOFT	

Ferrari waited till Tuesday before the race to decide on the constructions of the tyres to use. That is partly because Bridgestone and Ferrari had not won in Monaco for the past three years. In the end, Ferrari chose 2 specifications of tyres which were the same compound but with different constructions. The latest construction was a development of the successful one, which was used in Imola, with improved traction. For the qualifying session and the race, Ferrari and Jordan chose to run the tyre specification with that latest construction while Minardi stayed with the older one. However Ferrari lacked much needed one lap performance when it counted, in the 1st qualifying session – they were more than 1 second slower than the time they were able to do in the morning and the Ferrari drivers were almost 2.5 seconds away from Raikkonen who was on the provisional pole. It was a different story after all in the race. Michael Schumacher clocked the fastest lap of the race and was able to finish in 7th position. Technical Manager of Bridgestone, Hisao Suganuma, confessed after the race that they should have brought a tyre which was a one step softer compound than the one used.

Europe

	Ferrari	Jordan	Minardi		Williams
HARD	MSC & RB	NK & TM	CA & PF	HARD	MW & N...
SOFT				SOFT	

The Japanese tyre manufacture came to Nurburgring with 3 specifications for its teams. Those tyres were previously used in racing conditions. It was an extremely hot weekend and thus all Bridgestone runners opted for hard tyres.- Ferrari and Jordan using the same specification and Minardi using a slightly different tyre. The qualifying format from the European Grand Prix was changed back to a single qualifying session but it did not change anything for Bridgestone runners.

Canada

	Ferrari	Jordan	Minardi		Williams
HARD	MSC & RB		CA	HARD	MW & N...
SOFT		NK & TM	PF	SOFT	

Bridgestone sent its staff 3 weeks prior to the Grand Prix to check out the newly re-paved track surface. The Bridgestone choices in Montreal were slightly harder than those used in Nurburgring – a similar strategy to the previous years. There were 4 specifications available. Two of them were totally new – including the hard compound that Ferrari had. Bridgestone also provided Ferrari with yet another new rear tyre construction for improved traction. Ferrari suffered from excessive graining with the soft compound; therefore they had to settle for the hard. However, there was some sign of improvement in one lap performance. In the race, Ferrari's choice proved fine and they managed a double podium finish for the first time in the season.

USA

	Ferrari	Jordan	Minardi		Williams
HARD		NK & TM	CA & PF	HARD	MW & N...
SOFT	MSC & RB			SOFT	

For Indianapolis, Bridgestone brought 4 different specifications which included 1 compound. Ferrari chose the soft specification tyre they used as the hard specification one week ago in Montreal. Jordan and Minardi opted to use the harder specification. Bridgestone checked all of their tyres after witnessing the incidents by the Michelin runners, but confirmed that they experienced no problems.

France

	Ferrari	Jordan	Minardi		Williams
HARD		NK & TM	CA & PF	HARD	MW & N...
SOFT	MSC & RB			SOFT	

Bridgestone brought 5 compounds which included the latest ones. All compounds came from the medium to soft range. In the end, Ferrari chose the latest soft compound and Jordan and Minardi settled for the hard which was previously used. The tyres that Ferrari used showed better one-lap performance which they lacked to a certain extent in the previous races. However, it was not that effective on race day. Hirohide Hamashima admitted to a lack of grip and said that the new compound needed more developing.

Great Britain

	Ferrari	Jordan	Minardi		Williams
HARD	MSC & RB			HARD	
SOFT		NK & TM	CA & PF	SOFT	MW & N...

Silverstone has a very abrasive track surface therefore tyres from the harder sector of the compound range are required. Bridgestone had 4 specifications available including new compounds from the harder sector of its compound range. It was surprising that the Japanese decided not to bring any of the compounds that they tested at the same venue 5 weeks before. Ferrari settled for the hard but they got the tyre pressure wrong (3 psi higher than it should have been) on Michael Schumacher's left rear for his qualifying run, therefore he was only 10th on the grid. Barrichello qualified 6th but it showed again that the Ferrari and Bridgestone combination lost one-lap performance to a certain degree. The race pace of the hard tyres that Ferrari chose was consistent but could not match the pace of top Michelin users.

Germany

	Ferrari	Jordan	Minardi		Williams
HARD	RB	NK & TM		HARD	
SOFT	MSC		CA & RD	SOFT	MW & N...

Bridgestone brought 4 specifications and some of them were the latest compound developments from the latest family of compounds which aimed at improving qualifying performance while keeping the race consistency. The soft specification that Ferrari had was the one which was tested in Paul Ricard the previous week. Michael Schumacher qualified 5th with the soft, but it was first thought a little marginal to cover the race distance after reviewing its wear rate. Barrichello went for the hard which was used in the previous GPs. As it was feared, Michael Schumacher lost the grip as the race went on, and eventually finished 5th.

Hungary

	Ferrari	Jordan	Minardi		Williams
HARD			CA & RD	HARD	
SOFT	MSC & RB	NK & TM		SOFT	MW & N...

Bridgestone provided 6 specifications of tyres for its teams. This meant that the every team had its own choices. The soft compound that Ferrari had was something new and different that the Japanese tyre supplier requested from its technical centre in Tokyo after the disappointment in Germany, which arrived at the track on Wednesday night. The effort paid off to certain extent since Michael Schumacher, who used the latest soft specification, was considerably quicker than anyone else in the qualifying session and achieved his first pole of the year. The race was the same old story for Bridgestone and Ferrari. Michael Schumacher opted for a three stop strategy like the other top runners during the race, but his tyres started to lose their edge in the second stint. Michael Schumacher finished second. It was an encouraging race for Bridgestone and Ferrari.

Turkey

	Ferrari	Jordan	Minardi		Williams
HARD	MSC & RB		CA & RD	HARD	MW & N...
SOFT		NK & TM		SOFT	

Bridgestone had sent engineers to the track prior to the race. The Japanese firm brought 4 specifications altogether from their medium to hard compound range after doing lots of simulation work and found the track long and fast, putting a high load on the tyres. After the first day of running, Ferrari found that the soft tyres were too soft and would only last 30+ laps wear-wise. They anticipated the track surface would be less abrasive once it got rubbered in but they had no choice but to go for the hard compound which was race-proven, but it seemed too hard. Jordan opted for the soft compound and Minardi chose the hard but the tyres that these two teams chose were identical. In the end, Hirohide Hamashima concluded the tyres that Ferrari used were 'about two steps harder than it should have been'.

Italy

	Ferrari	Jordan	Minardi		Williams
HARD				HARD	
SOFT	MSC & RB	NK & TM	CA & RD	SOFT	MW & A...

After three days of testing during the previous week, Bridgestone brought 3 compounds. Two of them were well proven ones and the other was new. The new construction was introduced for Monza because of the track's high speed nature, and was the same for every team. All Bridgestone runners opted to use the softer compounds, but Ferrari used the latest one while Jordan and Minardi chose the older one. Michael Schumacher's pace in the race was 1.0 – 1.2 sec. slower than the race winner Montoya. It was revealed that the Japanese tyre manufacturer could not provide any compounds softer than the ones they used as Ross Brawn admitted that Ferrari and Bridgestone had even tried the Hungarian specification in the testing but it blistered.

Belgium

	Ferrari	Jordan	Minardi		Williams
HARD	MSC & RB			HARD	
SOFT		NK & TM	CA & RD	SOFT	MW & A...

Bridgestone brought 5 specifications to Spa-Francorchamps where the weather is always unpredictable. Traditionally Bridgestone brought compounds from their medium to hard range because of the relatively rough track surface and the high speed nature of Spa, but this time, they brought all the tyres from the medium range so the compounds used were similar to the ones seen in Magny Cours and Nurburgring. It was not that the Soft tyres were too soft, but In the end Ferrari opted to run the Hard compound because it gave them better car balance. The other two teams chose to run the soft but theirs were slightly different from the one brought for Ferrari. As anticipated, the race was run in wet to damp conditions. The Bridgestone camp was in fairly confident mood, but Hamashima admitted that the wetter the track was, it would be better for their products, and damp to drying conditions would not be preferable. The Ferrari drivers started the race on the standard wets (intermediates), but Michael Schumacher came in and changed to the dry during the safety car period, but the track was still too wet, therefore he came back in for the wet on the next lap. On the other hand, Barrichello stayed with the wets until the late stage of the race, and it proved to be the right decision. He finished 5th. Tiago Monteiro was another Bridgestone driver who finished in the points.

Brazil

	Ferrari	Jordan	Minardi		Williams
HARD		NK	CA & RD	HARD	
SOFT	MSC & RB	TM		SOFT	MW & A...

There were 4 compounds for Interlagos track from the soft to medium range. As usual the track was green, and there was some graining seen with the softer specifications on the front right tyres as well as the rears at the beginning of the weekend. but as the track was rubbered in, the problem ceased. The three drivers, Michael Schumacher, Barrichello, and Monteiro, opted to run the same soft. Katrhikeyan, Albers, and Monteiro went for the hard. The Ferrari drivers had a reasonable race with Schumacher finishing 4th and Barrichello came home in 6th.

Japan

	Ferrari	Jordan	Minardi		Williams
HARD				HARD	
SOFT	MSC & RB	NK & TM	CA & RD	SOFT	MW & A...

Bridgestone brought 3 different specifications. The Japanese tyre manufacture tested new specifications in Mugello prior to the Grand Prix, but they were not convinced with the performance, therefore the tyres in Suzuka were all well race-proven ones. Michelin suspected that one of the compounds that Bridgestone brought was the one that the Japanese company used at Suzuka in 2004. Although the changeable weather hampered the team's amount of running, Bridgestone shod teams all selected soft dry tyres in the end. Also Bridgestone's extreme wet tyres performed well in Free Practice session, but as far as standard wets (intermediates) were concerned, it was clear they did not have the speed advantage which they once enjoyed over the Michelin's counter part.

China

	Ferrari	Jordan	Minardi		Williams
HARD				HARD	
SOFT	MSC & RB	NK & TM	CA & RD	SOFT	MW & N...

For the Shanghai race, Bridgestone provided 4 specifications for its teams. Bridgestone's choices of compounds were all from the soft to medium range. The new compound was brought but it was never selected to race. There were no problems with the wear rates and heat durability, it was down to just two soft specifications which were the same as the ones in Hungary in the end. Again Ferrari chose to run the slightly different compound from Jordan or Minardi. For Ferrari and Bridgestone, it was rather suiting end to the disappointing season. Michael Schumacher collided with Minardi's Christijan Albers on the reconnaissance lap, forcing both to start from the pit lane in spare cars. Then the Ferrari driver skidded off the track on the cold tyres during the safety car period.

MICHELIN

cLaren R & JPM	**Renault** GF & FA	**BAR** JB & TS	**Toyota** JT & RSC	**Red Bull** CK & DC	**Sauber** FM JV	2005 was the year that drivers had to use a single set of tyres for all of the qualifying sessions and a full race distance. Michelin brought 3 different compounds to Albert Park. Those tyres were tested in Jerez in February before the Grand Prix. There were two compounds as the Prime (Hard) and one as the Option (Soft). Toyota and Williams were the only teams who had the harder Prime compound. Every team opted to use the softer of the two that they had, except for Toyota. Toyota chose the hardest compound because they anticipated graining with the soft. Pierre Dupasquier assessed the result as satisfactory, but he thought that the French tire manufacture should have brought an even softer compound for the race.
cLaren R & JPM	**Renault** GF & FA	**BAR** JB & AD	**Toyota** JT & RSC	**Red Bull** CK & DC	**Sauber** FM & JV	There were only 2 different dry-weather compounds available for Sepang. After testing in Jerez, most teams changed their option (soft) compound to the one which was originally designed for Bahrain since it proved better, and all the teams opted to run this compound. The track temperatures went up well above 50 degrees centigrade, but despite the conditions the tyres performed mostly well. McLaren encountered problems although it was not Michelin's fault. Montoya suffered from a flat-spotted tyre and Raikkonen had a puncture on his right rear due to a tyre valve failure.
cLaren R & PDR	**Renault** GF & FA	**BAR** JB & TS	**Toyota** JT & RSC	**Red Bull** CK & DC	**Sauber** FM JV	Michelin again brought only 2 compounds of tyres to Bahrain. The Option (Soft) compound was designed especially for the track but the Prime (hard) compound was the one all the teams had run as the Option in Malaysia. The tyre construction was new for both front and rear, but Renault chose to run the old front tyre construction for the sake of better balance. The new rear tyre construction improved traction out of slow corners and reduced the wear at the same time. Most drivers except for the two from BAR and Massa ended up using the Option. BAR decided to go conservative after anglicizing the wear rate of tyres and the lap times which showed a large drop-off after the 2nd lap. All Michelin users finished in the points.
cLaren R & AW	**Renault** GF & FA	**BAR** JB & TS	**Toyota** JT & RSC	**Red Bull** VL & DC	**Sauber** FM & JV	For Imola, the French tyre manufacture brought 5 different compounds that were all new. There were 3 Primes (hard) and 2 Options (soft). McLaren and Toyota chose the softest of 5 compounds available and the rest chose the tyre, which was one step harder than those two teams. On the race day, the ambient and track temperatures were cooler than anticipated and the difference in those two specifications was not visible. Although Alonso won the race, Michelin shod teams lost a bit of pace during the second and third stints. The wear rate was a little higher than expected.
cLaren R & JPM	**Renault** GF & FA	**BAR** DNP DNP	**Toyota** JT & RSC	**Red Bull** VL & DC	**Sauber** FM & JV	Michelin decided to bring 3 different compounds and 2 different front constructions (the old one for Renault) to the Circuit de Catalunya. This led to a total of 5 different specifications of tyres. When the teams chose the two specifications prior to the race, the weather forecasts suggested cloudy and cool conditions, therefore the two specifications which had a lower temperature working range were designated as the Primes for this race. Toyota was the only team who had the softer of the Prime compounds. Consequently, the compound for the Option had a higher temperature working range. All the teams chose to run the Primes because of their performance and cooler weather was anticipated for the race day. However it turned out to be sunny and warm. Many teams experienced a little bit of blistering, but it was not a serious problem.
cLaren R & JPM	**Renault** GF & FA	**BAR** DNP DNP	**Toyota** JT & RSC	**Red Bull** VL & DC	**Sauber** FM & JV	Michelin had 3 compounds available for Monaco. The teams had two kinds of Prime (Hard) to choose from, and just one kind of Option (soft) which was the same for everybody. Williams was the only one who had the harder Prime tyre and the rest of the teams including Renault had the softer Prime tyre, although Michelin claimed that there was not much difference between them. Most teams opted to run the Option tyre for the better grip but Williams opted for the Prime as did Renault. Raikkonen started from the pole and won the race easily. On the other hand the two Renault drivers, who initially ran 2nd and 3rd, suffered severe degradation on their rears and lost the pace in the second half of the race. Their cars proved to be harder on the rear tyres than those of some rival teams. It was to such an extent that Pat Symonds had to admit after the race "It exceeded even our most pessimistic predictions."
cLaren R & JPM	**Renault** GF & FA	**BAR** JB & TS	**Toyota** JT & RSC	**Red Bull** VL & DC	**Sauber** FM & JV	Michelin brought 4 compounds - 3 types of Primes and 1 type of Option.- for Nurburgring. All the Prime compounds were the same ones seen in Imola. Again, there were two kinds of front tyre construction. The new rear construction was carried over from Monaco, but only the Option adopted the new construction. Interestingly McLaren had the hardest Prime and BAR had the softest Prime. In the end, McLaren and BAR settled for the Option (soft) along with Toyota, Redbull, and Sauber while Williams and Renault (who were hard on rear tyres) went for the Prime. Both specifications performed well in the race, but the race leader Raikkonen crashed on the last lap of the race due to a suspension failure that was caused by a flat-spotted tyre.
cLaren R & JPM	**Renault** GF & FA	**BAR** JB & TS	**Toyota** JT & RSC	**Red Bull** CK & DC	**Sauber** FM & JV	Michelin came to Montreal with 3 compounds - 2 types of Primes and 1 type of Option. McLaren and Toyota had the softer Prime compound which was believed to be new. The other five teams had the Prime which was raced in Nurburgring by Renault and Williams. Also the Option was the same as the one that appeared in Germany 2 weeks before. All specifications used the new rear construction which had been introduced in Bahrain. All three compounds were used in the race, and the 2 McLaren drivers showed speed and consistency with the softest compound.
cLaren R & JPM	**Renault** GF & FA	**BAR** JB & TS	**Toyota** JT & RSC	**Red Bull** CK & DC	**Sauber** FM & JV	It was an embarrassing weekend for Michelin as their teams had to withdraw from the race for safety reasons after tyre failures in practice. It all started on Friday when Ralf Schumacher crashed his Toyota at the final turn due to a left rear tyre failure. This was followed by another tyre failure which happened to Richardo Zonta's Toyota. Michelin had just two types of tyres available at Indianapolis, one Prime and one Option for all the teams. The Prime compound was similar in range to the one used by Toyota in Montreal, and Ralf was on this tyre at the time of his accident. Zonta was on the Option tyres when he suffered his tyre failure. It was believed that the only teams who did not suffer any problems with the tyres were Williams and BAR. After the intensive examination of the tyres which had been run in the free practice sessions, Michelin concluded that they could not guarantee the safety of the drivers with those 2 types of tyres. Pierre Dupasquier explained the reason for the failure as pressure related but emphasized that their tyres were not intrinsically flawed, but were insufficiently suited to the extreme racing conditions encountered through the final corner. Michelin tried to convince the FIA to allow them to use a new (Barcelona) specification tyre that could have arrived in time for the race, but the governing body claimed that would be in breach of the regulations. Michelin-shod teams also asked for an extra chicane to be installed before the final high-speed banked turn, but the request was rejected by the FIA. The seven Michelin teams had no options but to pull out of the race after the formation lap.
cLaren PM R	**Renault** GF & FA	**BAR** JB TS	**Toyota** JT & RSC	**Red Bull** CK & DC	**Sauber** FM JV	Although there were two types of tyre constructions available, all the Michelin teams selected the same two compound choices from the medium range for the French tyre manufacture's home race. Those compounds were both new and from a different family. The softer tyre had a slight edge in the qualifying session, but tyre choices were down to the drivers preference since there were no worries about wear rates whichever tyre you had chosen. Softer compound tyres were used by the Renault drivers, Toyota drivers, Raikkkonen, Sato, and Villeneuve. The rest opted to go with the harder compound. Both compounds proved to be quick in the race but Trulli's Toyota experienced huge tyre performance drop-off as the race went on.
cLaren R & JPM	**Renault** GF & FA	**BAR** JB & TS	**Toyota** RSC JT	**Red Bull** CK & DC	**Sauber** FM & JV	There were 4 compounds available at Silverstone, they were from the harder end of the range but it was interesting how Michelin teams decided on the 2 choices prior to the Grand Prix. Most teams had the combination of the softer Prime compound and the harder Option compound. However, McLaren chose two of the softest, meaning they chose the same Option compound as the others and one more Option compound which was even softer. On the other hand Toyota requested the harder Prime and the same Option as the others. In the end, all the Michelin drivers, except for Ralf Schumacher, chose to run the same Option compound (which is hard for McLaren). According to Toyota, both specifications had merits and de-merits, they left the tyre choice to the drivers preference.
cLaren R & JPM	**Renault** GF & FA	**BAR** JB & TS	**Toyota** JT & RSC	**Red Bull** CK & DC	**Sauber** FM & JV	There were 3 kinds of Primes (hard) specifications and just 1 type of Option (soft) specification available in Hockenheim from the French company. Actually the hard or soft did not simply mean hard or soft for those tyres. The tyres Michelin had differed in the propensity to blister. In the end, because of the cooler temperatures of the weekend, which helped the wear rate, all Michelin shod cars opted for the Option which provided better grip.
cLaren R & JPM	**Renault** GF & FA	**BAR** JB & TS	**Toyota** JT & RSC	**Red Bull** CK & DC	**Sauber** FM & JV	Although Hungaroring is relatively slow, Michelin brought 3 compounds from the soft to medium range because of high ambient temperatures. There were 2 kinds of Primes and just 1 type of Option available. Both Prime specifications were the ones which had been available to McLaren and Toyota in Hockenheim a week before. The Prime that Williams, Redbull, and Sauber had were slightly harder than the one the rest of the Michelin runners had. For the qualifying session and the race, Renault and BAR chose the Prime specification and the other teams stayed with the Option specification. The ambient and track temperatures were similar to those of the Saturday afternoon, however, as it turned out, the choice made by Renault and BAR was wrong. They struggled for the grip in the race.
cLaren R & JPM	**Renault** GF & FA	**BAR** JB & TS	**Toyota** JT & RSC	**Red Bull** CK & DC	**Sauber** FM & JV	Michelin engineers visited the Istanbul Park track to inspect the track surface characteristics, along with their usual pre-race simulations with the partner teams. Since it was a new venue for Formula One, Michelin took 2 race-proven tyre specifications with broader operational spectrum to minimise the risk. Many teams found the wear rate of the soft specification high on Friday, and in the end, all the teams settled for the hard. Although some drivers complained the tyres worked only within a narrow temperature range, Michelin runners were generally quicker than Ferrari. It should be noted that Williams suffered three tyre failures during the race, but it was a car related problem rather than a tyre problem.
cLaren R & JPM	**Renault** GF & FA	**BAR** JB & TS	**Toyota** JT & RSC	**Red Bull** CK & DC	**Sauber** FM & JV	Michelin brought 5 different compounds to Monza, 4 compounds as the Primes (Hard) and 1 as the Option (Soft). Although there was not much difference between the Prime compounds, it is believed that Williams, Toyota, Redbull and Sauber had the hardest, BAR had the second hardest, Renault had the one which was slightly softer than BAR and McLaren had the softest Prime compound. In the end, all Michelin runners settled for soft compounds. It should be noted that McLaren and Renault used different construction which was originally designed for Spa-Francorchamps. McLaren's Montoya won the race but the team experienced tyre problems. Both Montoya and teammate Raikkonen's tyres suffered blisters on the outer edge of their rear tyres. It was believed that McLaren had put too much positive camber on the rear. Despite this, Pierre Dupasquier said after the race that they could have brought even softer tyres than the Option specification that was used.
cLaren R & JPM	**Renault** GF & FA	**BAR** JB & TS	**Toyota** JT & RSC	**Red Bull** DC CK	**Sauber** FM & JV	As Nick Shorrock, director of Michelin F1 activities, said "This was the race we have wanted for some time, " the race in Belgium was a wet affair. As far as dry tyres were concerned, Michelin brought 2 types of Primes (hard) tyres and just 1 type of Option (soft) tyre. McLaren, BAR, Sauber and Redbull's Coulthard chose the harder Prime compound which was used in Hockenheim and Hungaroring. The Prime compound that Renault used was slightly softer than the one McLaren and co. used but it was also seen in the German and Hungarian tracks as well. Williams, Toyota, and Klien ended up using the Option compound. All the tyres used 'The Spa construction' to withstand significant loads that tyres experience at Eau Rouge. Because of the rain, which came before the start, the track was wet at the start. So all Michelin runners took the standard wets (intermediates) to start with. The rain stopped as the race got under way, some drivers took a gamble to switch to the dry tyres when the safety car was deployed on lap 11, but as Nick Shorrock said after the race "The decision to use intermediates throughout - in wet and drying conditions - was the best option." Although Michelin dominated the top 5 positions in the race, the performance of the wet tyres from the both manufactures were evenly matched. Up untill last year, Michelin's dry tyres were very quick in the damp conditions. However, since the 2005 dry tyres had to last for a whole race, they were relatively hard and even the Option (soft) tyres could not handle the damp track well.
cLaren R & JPM	**Renault** GF & FA	**BAR** JB & TS	**Toyota** JT RSC	**Red Bull** CK & DC	**Sauber** FM & JV	The French tyre manufacture had 3 compounds available for Interlagos. Those compounds were exactly the same as the ones used in Spa, meaning 2 Prime compounds and 1 Option compound. Williams, McLaren Renault, BAR, and Trulli (Toyota) opted to run the Primes, but McLaren's choice was one step harder than the other 5 remaining cars including both Redbulls, both Saubers and Ralf Schumacher who decided to use the Option (soft). Montoya led home Raikkonen, making it the first 1-2 by McLaren since the Australian GP in 2000, and Alonso came third to win the championship. Michelin won the driver's title for the fourth time.
cLaren R & JPM	**Renault** GF & FA	**BAR** JB & TS	**Toyota** JT & RSC	**Red Bull** CK DC	**Sauber** FM JV	Michelin brought 3 Prime (hard) tyres and 1 Option (soft) tyre. Because of the rain, warmer weather and green track condition were anticipated on the race day, so Redbull's Klien chose the hardest tyre available, and the 2 BAR drivers and Mass opted to run the second hardest Prive tyre. Both the McLarens and Renaults decided to go with the softest Prime tyre. Option tyres were rather suited for cooler temperatures, and Williams, Toyotas, Coulthard and Villeneuve chose the specification. Toyota thought the rear tyres would suffer with fairly large degradation and so they opted to go for a three stop strategy. Ralf Schumacher put the car on the pole, but their strategy did not work out in the race because of the early safety-car period. Williams' Mark Webber did not have any problem at all with Option tyres. It was the first win for Michelin on Bridgestone's home ground.
cLaren R PM	**Renault** GF & FA	**BAR** JB & TS	**Toyota** JT & RSC	**Red Bull** CK & DC	**Sauber** FM & JV	For the season finale in Shanghai, there were 2 Prime (hard) compounds and just 1 Option (soft) compound available from the French company. The teams found that there was not a great deal of difference between the Prime and the Option compounds. Retiring Pierre Dupasquier put the reason down to "a by-product of the unexpectedly cool track temperatures." Both specifications showed no sign of graining, so all the drivers except for Raikkonen chose to use the Option tyres. The track temperature did not reach as high a level as Michelin had anticipated but the tyres worked well in both the qualifying session and the race. Alonso managed to snatch the 100th pole position for Michelin and ran away without handing the lead to anybody.

BRAKES

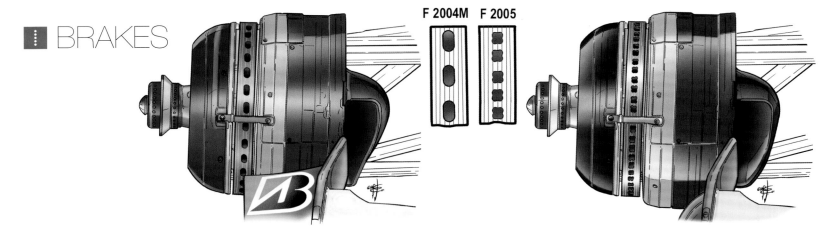

F 2004M   F 2005

The substantial aerodynamic modifications that came in with the 2005 technical regulations that especially concerned a reduction in vertical load, consequently curtailed the amount of work carried out by the cars' braking systems, especially in the first part of the season, when that reduction in relation to 2004 was more evident. On the other hand, the need to optimise the dimensions of the brake air intakes, the width of which notably influenced aerodynamics, forced most teams to invest time and resources in improving brake plant cooling and that involved both the ventilation of the discs (see Ferrari) and the design of the calipers. We even saw smaller, more efficient air intakes in 2005 and these were further integrated into the aerodynamics of the front end of the cars. The most important new development was Brembo's braking system designed jointly with Ferrari, which had a means of ventilation integrated between the disc, caliper and external aerodynamic drum, the result of considerable research by both companies. The use of this new development was immediately evident in Bahrain from the new shape of the air vents, which were smaller and closer together and were, moreover, created using a new technique. The new caliper was less evident, integrated as it was with an air intake specifically for cooling the component: its dimensions resulted from a great deal of research into thermo-fluid dynamics, which took into account the effective flow of air available in the front of the car.

FERRARI: DISC COMPARISON

The new development of sophisticated vents for the Brembo discs fitted to the F2005 is compared to the traditional units of the F2004 M. Those vents, which were smaller and closer to each other, seemed to result from a combination of four mini vents with more uneven edges, so as to create internal turbulence, and were the result of a profound analysis of internal fluid dynamics.
The ability to maintain the brake caliper at the best operating temperature and, therefore, to

be able to avoid overheating the brake fluid, brought with it a perceptible increase in the system's rigidity and a consistency of performance.
Each team supplied by Brembo integrated the cooling of the caliper into the design of the air intake. It should be remembered that a Formula One car's braking system is cooled solely by the car's dynamic air intake.
Due to the noted aerodynamic limitations, it was decided to discontinue the UHD (ultra-heavy duty) "heavy" caliper in 2005 and adopt the HD (heavy duty) unit, which was widened so that it could accommodate maximum width discs and pads of 28 mm and 25 mm respectively. In addition, the LD (light duty) caliper was used increasingly, due to the reduced width of the carbon fibre material used by Toyota (see the 2004 Technical Analysis) and now others on all the circuits in which wear was not a problem.

CANADA: BRAKE ANALYSIS OF THE GRAND PRIX

The Montreal track is, historically, the most severe on a car's braking system – even more so than Imola – where brakes are subjected to extremely violent and compacted stress due to the presence of no fewer than seven major braking points. That it is why is useful to analyse the braking systems used by the various teams during the Canadian weekend.
The complete resurfacing of the circuit reduced grip, making adherence less stressful for the braking systems in relation to previous seasons, when the outcome of the race was often dictated by the effectiveness of a car's brakes. The most violent and important braking point on the track is the fifth, the one that leads to the hairpin bend: the cars arrive there at 308 km/h in sixth gear to go into the corner at 120 km/h in second and drop to 65 km/h in first in a little under four seconds, producing a deceleration of 4G at the centre of the bend: they then exit the corner in the same gear at 107 km/h. A Formula One car goes from 100 km/h to 0 km/h in about 17 metres and takes about 2.5 seconds to do so. The peak tem-

perature of the discs climbs to over 1100° and for that reason it is extremely important to develop the right cooling intake system for the brakes. The biggest intakes were, perhaps, introduced by Williams, followed by BAR and Renault, while McLaren surprisingly brought in new ones at the front end with their section notably reduced in relation to those of 2004. Ferrari and BAR carried out experiments with disc brakes supplied by two different manufacturers: the two Maranello drivers tried both, while the British-based team had Sato alone test discs made by Carbon Industrie of France. And it was from the latter that the most important feedback came with the use of a brand new material for the discs and pads made for McLaren and Williams. The project started almost immediately after the 2004 Grand Prix of Canada and required a long testing period. That sophisticated solution was introduced especially for the Montreal circuit and was not used at any other track, not even Monza, which is also hard on the brakes. The other new development concerning the French manufacturer, which was fairly easy to notice, was the surprise supply of its brake discs to Ferrari. A choice that stupefied everyone, given that the F2005 was born around a project carried out exclusively with Brembo: this new move entailed Maranello's supply of the designs to the French firm to create the same special typology of vents.

In braking system terms, the Canadian grid was divided in this way:
CALIPERS: Brembo - Ferrari, Sauber, Toyota, Minardi. AP - McLaren, Williams, Renault, Red Bull and Jordan. ALCON - BAR.
DISCS: Brembo – Schumacher's Ferrari and the two BARs. Carbon Industrie - McLaren, Williams, Sauber, Red Bull and Barrichello's Ferrari. Hitco - Renault, Toyota, Jordan and Minardi.

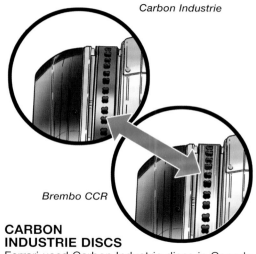
Carbon Industrie

Brembo CCR

CARBON INDUSTRIE DISCS

Ferrari used Carbon Industrie discs in Canada and at Monza instead of those of Brembo, although it should be said that only Barrichello did so at Montreal. We should also point out that Maranello supplied the exclusive designs of the air vents to the French company. The two discs can be easily distinguished from each other by the difference in the colour of the materials from which they are made. The CCR of the Italian manufacturer has feint lines, which can even be picked out at a distance.

AKEBONO CALIPERS

BAR surprised many at the Grand Prix of Japan by testing brake calipers made by the local manufacturer Akebono instead of its usual Alkon, which the team used exclusively in 2004. They, too, could be easily recognised by the gold coloured athermic protection on the inner part of the caliper.

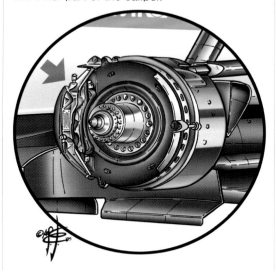

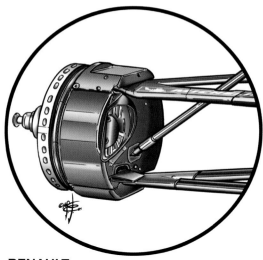

RENAULT

The Renault brake air intake was highly traditional and had no drums or other aerodynamic faring outside the disc, which all the other teams had used with either more or less sophisticated features.

NEW TENDENCIES

Up until the 2004 season, the double drum feature introduced by Ferrari – first an internal version on the F2001 and then an external on the F2003 GA – created a trend. But with the ban on tyre changes during a race, this technique, which was considered advantageous to the exploitation of the car's aerodynamics, was progressively abandoned in favour of faring that only partially covered the brake discs for improved thermal dissipation. It was McLaren that first came up with this new approach on the MP4-19B, which was continued on the MP4-20, then BAR and Minardi took it up. Williams and Toyota went further still during the last races of the season, covering the entire vertical air vent of the discs radial ducts in carbon fibre. In practice, Williams had even made a second shell (2) that wrapped around the internal one (1) of the Ferrari school. The hot air shot towards the outside in the central part of the rim. This was a solution that tended to ensure the heat of the brakes did not interfere with the tyres through the wheels overheating and, subsequently, with the endurance of the tyres. A feature that may be further developed, due to the return of tyre changes during the Grands Prix.

Ferrari 2001

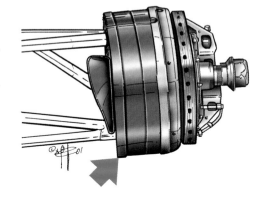

Williams

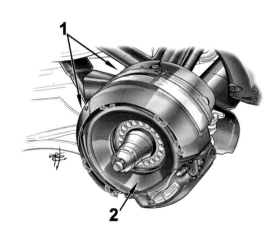

McLaren 2004

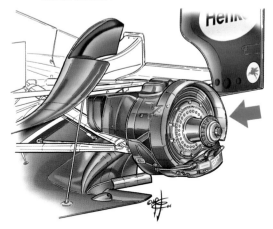

Toyota

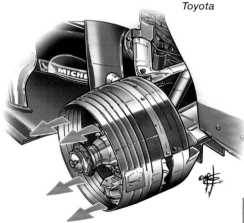

TALKING ABOUT AERODYNAMICS

On the aerodynamics front, the teams' task was to interpret the new package of technical rules for 2005, which brought with them restrictions regarded by everyone as the most radical of the last decade, especially the harsh aerodynamic limitations that affected the principal sectors of the car, to which was added the obligation of using a single set of tyres for the whole race. The immediate loss of downforce caused by the new rules, recorded during winter testing of the "hybrid" cars, was of the order of 22-25%, which had been cut to a little less than 15% by the start of the championship and was further diminished during the season by additional development carried out in that area by all the top teams. The

general tendency was to search for the maximum downforce and the minimum variation of dynamic handling, whereas in 2004 aerodynamic efficiency was privileged after a period of regulation

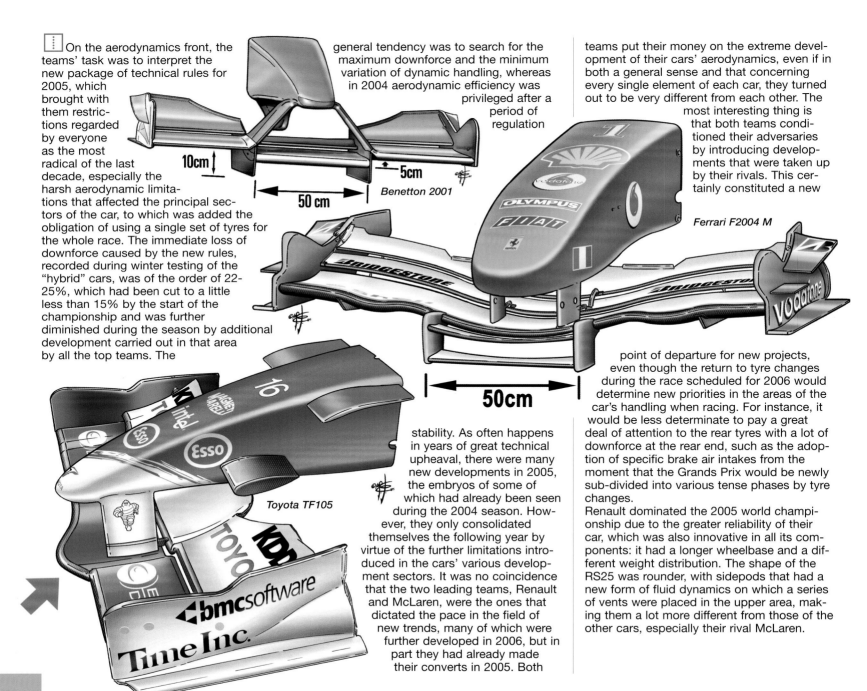

Benetton 2001

10cm
5cm
50 cm

Ferrari F2004 M

50cm

Toyota TF105

stability. As often happens in years of great technical upheaval, there were many new developments in 2005, the embryos of some of which had already been seen during the 2004 season. However, they only consolidated themselves the following year by virtue of the further limitations introduced in the cars' various development sectors. It was no coincidence that the two leading teams, Renault and McLaren, were the ones that dictated the pace in the field of new trends, many of which were further developed in 2006, but in part they had already made their converts in 2005. Both

teams put their money on the extreme development of their cars' aerodynamics, even if in both a general sense and that concerning every single element of each car, they turned out to be very different from each other. The most interesting thing is that both teams conditioned their adversaries by introducing developments that were taken up by their rivals. This certainly constituted a new

point of departure for new projects, even though the return to tyre changes during the race scheduled for 2006 would determine new priorities in the areas of the car's handling when racing. For instance, it would be less determinate to pay a great deal of attention to the rear tyres with a lot of downforce at the rear end, such as the adoption of specific brake air intakes from the moment that the Grands Prix would be newly sub-divided into various tense phases by tyre changes.
Renault dominated the 2005 world championship due to the greater reliability of their car, which was also innovative in all its components: it had a longer wheelbase and a different weight distribution. The shape of the RS25 was rounder, with sidepods that had a new form of fluid dynamics on which a series of vents were placed in the upper area, making them a lot more different from those of the other cars, especially their rival McLaren.

FRONT WINGS

The designers' first reaction was to recuperate as much vertical load as possible, after it had been diminished by further raising the front wing group by another 5 cm. Ferrari partially went back to the solution introduced by Benetton in 2001 at the time of the first reduction in the height of the front wing from the ground, creating a stepped area in the centre, in the 50 cm wide zone where, as permitted by legislation, it can be pushed as far as the height of the reference plane. This was a drastic move that guaranteed a good load value, but was penalised by a greater pitch sensitivity. Toyota's answer was along the same lines but was less radical, with the central part of their car's front wing heavily spoon shaped and inclined forward.

Prost Monaco 2001

Ferrari Sepang 2001

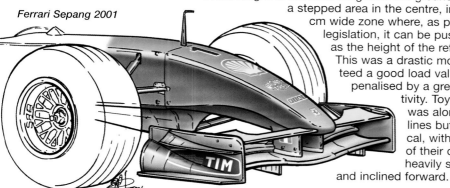

MONACO: TOYOTA

The search for maximum downforce led to this mini-plane, located inside the barge boards of the Toyota at Monaco: it was a variation on the double mini-flap theme brought in by Renault at Imola.

DOUBLE FLAP

Another technique from the past was the return of the double flap, which Barrichello used as far back as 2001 for a single lap in practice on the Friday morning during the Grand Prix of Malaysia. The feature, which appeared on the Prost from the Grand Prix of Monaco, was taken up in 2005 and used once more by Sauber, but only during private testing: it inspired the eventual raised mini-flap, introduced by Renault, which then became fashionable during the course of the season.

BUDAPEST: TOYOTA

Toyota and Williams arrived at Budapest with a series of three wings behind the engine air intake in place of the two-plane technique seen previously at Monaco, also in the preceding seasons. Those of Toyota fully exploited the permitted width of 60 cm.

RENAULT

At the Grand Prix of Hungary, Renault used a new rear wing with large serrated Gurney flaps that were bigger than those previously seen. Shown in yellow in the illustration, one of the Gurneys is linked to another flap with a straight trailing edge. The double mini-plane made a comeback above the rear light, introduced – but not used – at the Grand Prix of Canada. The end plates had vents of the Toyota school.

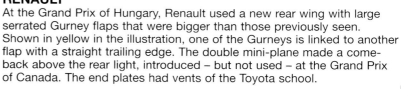

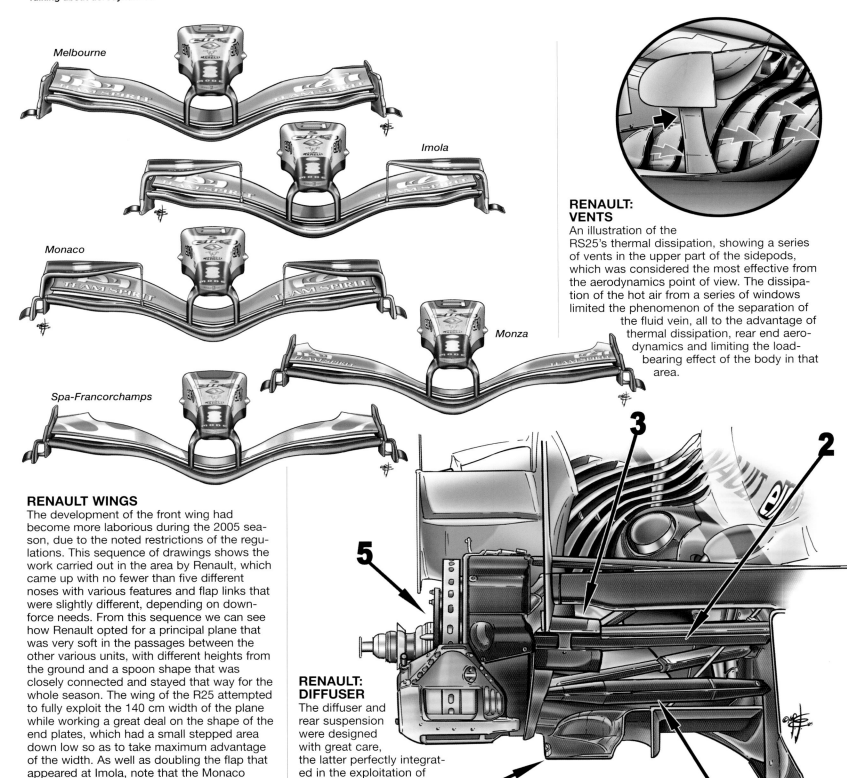

Melbourne

Imola

Monaco

Monza

Spa-Francorchamps

RENAULT: VENTS

An illustration of the RS25's thermal dissipation, showing a series of vents in the upper part of the sidepods, which was considered the most effective from the aerodynamics point of view. The dissipation of the hot air from a series of windows limited the phenomenon of the separation of the fluid vein, all to the advantage of thermal dissipation, rear end aerodynamics and limiting the load-bearing effect of the body in that area.

RENAULT WINGS

The development of the front wing had become more laborious during the 2005 season, due to the noted restrictions of the regulations. This sequence of drawings shows the work carried out in the area by Renault, which came up with no fewer than five different noses with various features and flap links that were slightly different, depending on downforce needs. From this sequence we can see how Renault opted for a principal plane that was very soft in the passages between the other various units, with different heights from the ground and a spoon shape that was closely connected and stayed that way for the whole season. The wing of the R25 attempted to fully exploit the 140 cm width of the plane while working a great deal on the shape of the end plates, which had a small stepped area down low so as to take maximum advantage of the width. As well as doubling the flap that appeared at Imola, note that the Monaco introduction of vents on the outside of the end plates was aimed at bettering the efficiency of the main plane. The raised double flap only remained unused on the fast circuits of Monza and Spa, being replace by the traditional unit with a tail and a much reduced incidence. It was combined with a spooned principal plane with a smaller variation of height.

RENAULT: DIFFUSER

The diffuser and rear suspension were designed with great care, the latter perfectly integrated in the exploitation of the car's rear end aerodynamics. The toe-in arms (1) had fairing with a much extended wing plane that acted as a diffuser for the lateral channels. (2) The drive shafts were only faired to the rear but had a large amount of fairing (3) about 15 cm wide in the area near the wheel, a feature that remained on the car for the entire season. A lot of refinement work was carried out in the sealing area (4) with the wheel, which was penalised by the new regulation restrictions.

UPPER DECK FLAP

Credit should be given to Renault for having introduced this feature, which not only permitted the recuperation of vertical load on the front end, but also improved the airflow towards the rear of the car, therefore producing greater rear wing efficiency. A technique that was later taken up by many teams during the season (see table).

TOYOTA: VENTS

And credit must also go to Toyota for bringing in a development a year in advance in Australia in 2004: it was the horizontal vents in the rear wing end plates, the purpose of which was to reduce the vortices created in that area, bringing an improvement in both the efficiency and downforce of the wing. All the teams gradually invoked similar features in 2006, the key examples of which are shown in the table. In some cases, like those of Renault and McLaren, the vents have only been used on circuits of maximum load; other teams made them an integral part of the wing group for almost all Grands Prix.

Williams

Ferrari

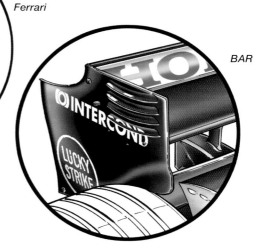

BAR

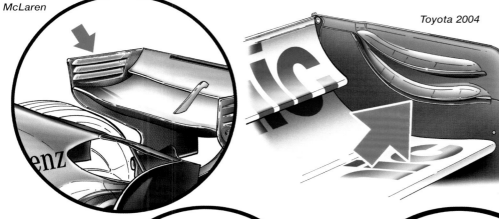

Toyota 2004

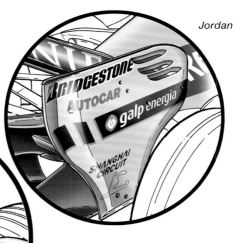

Jordan

McLaren

Renault

Red Bull

JAGUAR TREND

It is good to see that every now and then even the smaller teams have the ability to launch a fashion, which was the case with Minardi on many occasions with developments that were at the forefront of technology. In 2005, almost all the teams adopted a design trend instigated by Jaguar – a team bought by Red Bull – in 2004 and which became even more determinate due to the greater restrictions introduced by the Federation in the area around the rear wheels. It was the vertical fin, brought in to keep the air flow complete in the area inside the rear wheels. Present also on the Red Bull, these fins inspired most teams to go the same way: McLaren from the Grand Prix of Australia, Renault from Monaco, the two versions from Toyota, BAR with an added flap similar to the one on the Renault, as well as Williams and Minardi.

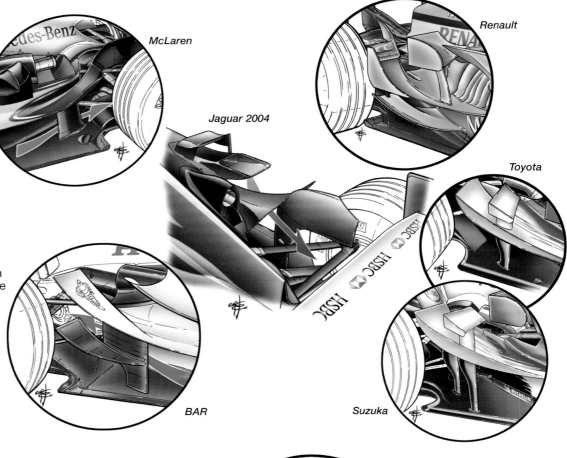

McLaren

Renault

Jaguar 2004

Toyota

BAR

Suzuka

Renault 2004

Williams

McLaren

Ferrari

Arrows

THE FORWARD EXTENSION OF THE BARGE BOARDS

Renault came to Monaco in 2004 with a small triangular fin angled forward, applied in the terminal area of the barge boards behind the wheels, which, in practice, acted as a front extension of the sidepods. A device the purpose of which was to render the air flow more energetic in that delicate zone that serves as a feed towards all the narrowing rear end and especially to the central channel of the diffuser. It was a development that converted all the teams a little, starting with BAR, the team that introduced it at the presentation of its 007 and was, obviously, on the RS25. During the season, just about all the teams converted to this development: Williams from the Grand Prix of Australia, Ferrari at Imola, McLaren at the Nurburgring, Jordan at Monza followed by the other cars, including Minardi.

38

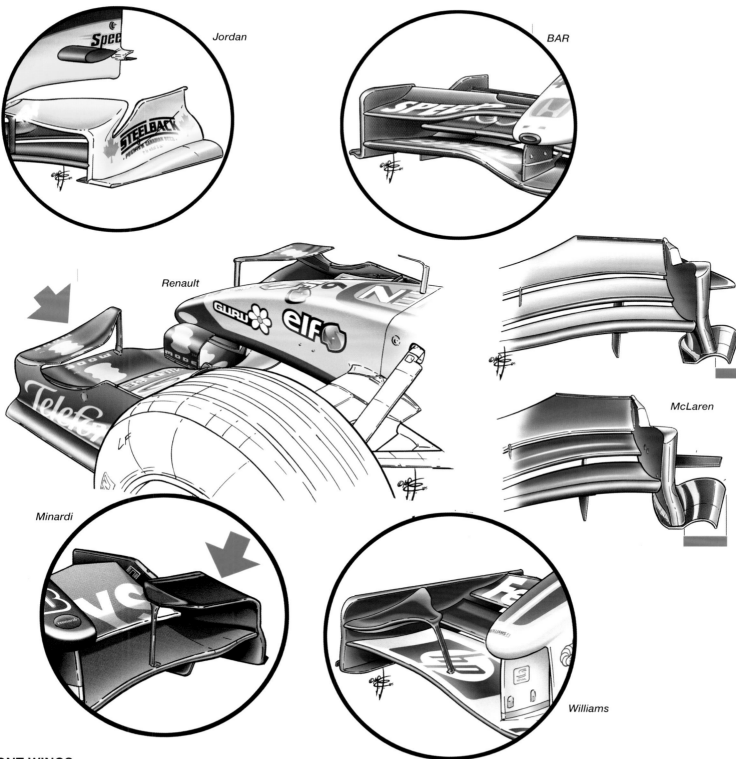

Jordan

BAR

Renault

McLaren

Minardi

Williams

FRONT WINGS

Raising the nose by another 5 cm demanded a notable re-examination of all the components and spawned many new developments. Two, in particular, became trends: Renault's upper deck flap at Imola and the new, more inward alignment of the end plates of McLaren. Rather than to generate an increase in load on the front end, the first influenced the air flow towards the car's body, increasing the efficiency of the rear wing.

This feature had already been copied by Jordan, BAR, Minardi and Williams during the 2005 season in the order shown in the summary table.

But at McLaren, there was a progressive alignment towards the inside of the end plates, giving up a large amount of the maximum 140 cm principal plane width to privilege air flow efficiency and better direct the air to the inside of the channels, delimited on the one side by the walls of the chassis and the other by the bulk of the tyres. This development was partially copied by Williams, BAR and Ferrari.

COCKPITS, PEDALS AND STEERING WHEELS

As with the 2004 season, in 2005 few of the teams made major modifications to their cars' cockpits or the shape of their steering wheels. Indeed, Williams-BMW used a wheel derived from another of two years earlier, but notably simplified as far as the number of paddles and its actual functions were concerned, especially due to the severe limitation of electronics regulations, particularly in automatic management of the start, which was in full effect in 2004 but was limited in 2005. Despite the fact that modification had reduced the enormous advantage Renault enjoyed in this area without reverting to such automation, the French car did better than all its rivals in the delicate start stage.

The same was the case with McLaren, which went back to having a display separate from the steering wheel - as they had in 2002 – on which the driver could see key information. The frequent mechanical problems that plagued the Anglo-German team permitted the analysis of their pedal shapes used by their drivers, generally scrupulously guarded in the pits. There were not even any new developments in this area, as all the drivers used the left foot braking system and separators between the two pedals to better block the ankles.

FERRARI STEERING WHEEL
The F2005 steering wheel was identical to the one on the F2004 in both shape and its number of paddles and buttons. The comparison is with the previous year's wheel, shown in black and white to better indicate how many of the buttons and paddles had different functions or had been moved in relation to the 2004 version, while the principal basic functions remained the same; the illustration shows the steering wheel used by Schumacher, while Barrichello's had slightly different positions for some of his controls.
(1) pit lane speed limiter; (2) buttons to activate the starting procedure, substantially limited by the severe regulation restrictions; (3) radio; (4-17) paddles for the management of the differential going into and coming out of corners, with the possibility of increasing or decreasing their effectiveness by the use of two specific buttons marked + and – high up on the sides of the crown of the wheel (see illustration below). On the 2004

steering wheel, those functions were activated by using paddle 18; (5) rev limiter with which to intervene on the engine's revolutions; (6) traction control; (7) drink button; (8) activation of management parameters in the presence of the safety car (the previous year, button 13 carried out this function; (9) diverse management of engine revs (in 2004, this button controlled the supplementary oil pump); (10) spare button; (11) button for switching off the engine; (12) control with which to activate the mechanical oil pump in case of necessity (switched places in 2004 with the management of the functions in the presence of the safety car); (13) differential management; (15) mechanical fuel cap opener, when needed; (14) diverse parameters for operating the clutch; (16) activation of the back-up strategy for clutch management (the previous year, this

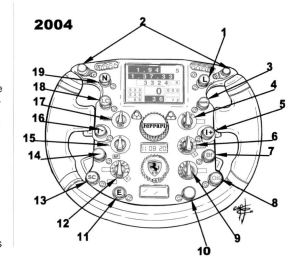

2004

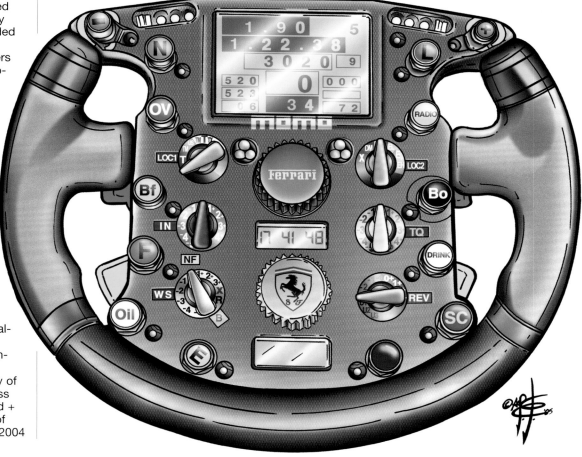

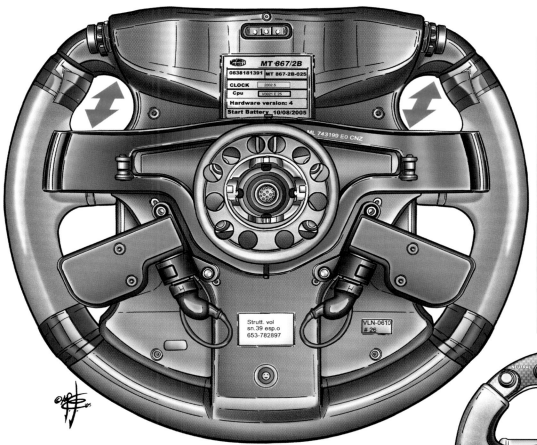

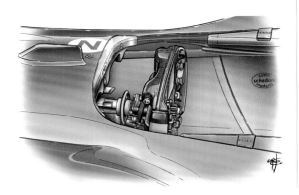

RENAULT

The French constructor's steering wheel was unchanged, the only new item the insertion of the of a paddle at the sides of the central part above right, indicated with a red arrow, with which to select from the various programmes. There are only four paddles of the right on the left that govern the traction control, clutch, accelerator and the air/fuel blend, while all the other functions are carried out by using the large central paddle, which selects all the different programmes; it is then up to the driver to define the typology of the intervention by operating another control.

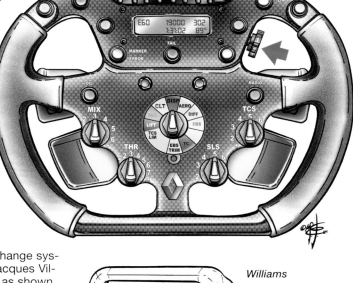

was the number 7 button, now the one with which the driver could go deeper into the information on the display; (17) second paddle for managing the differential (see number 4); (18) over revving indicator should such a condition occur; (19) neutral inserter. The reverse gear button is protected and located to the left of the steering wheel in the cockpit hoop. The lights high up are to signal the correct revs to use during gear changes and to alert the driver to an anomaly; in such a case, the lighted signal is accompanied by a message on the display. The two large black and grey paddles enable the driver to vary the information he sees on the display.

FERRARI

At the sides, high up in the crown of the steering wheel are two buttons with which to rapidly increase or decrease the management of some programmes, especially in crucial phases of a race: they were previously numbers 5 and 16 on the wheel, as shown in the black and white illustration relative to 2004.

FERRARI LIKE VILLENEUVE

Ferrari adopted a one hand gear change system, which was always used by Jacques Villeneuve at both Williams and BAR as shown in the illustration. The only major difference was that the Canadian operated the system solely with his right hand, pushing or pulling the rocker towards or away from himself, while the Ferrari drivers used both hands. The management rocker is a single and no longer split element. Its two-way movement controls both operations. Pulling the rocker towards himself with his right hand the driver changes up, while carrying out the same movement with the left hand he changes down. Pushing the rocker forward with the right hand changes down and with the left up. This disposition was dictated by the fact that Schumacher usually operated his brakes balance paddle with his right hand, which is on the right at the side of the steering wheel.

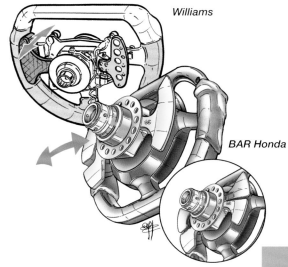

Williams

BAR Honda

2001

2005

FERRARI TELEVISION CAMERA

This has nothing to do with the technical side of the car, but it is interesting to note the installation of tiny television cameras inside the mirrors, which, for this reason, were the cause of a number of breakages. That just shows how carefully every element is designed today as part of an F1 car that is taken to the absolute limit of its functional capability.

JORDAN

Jordan was one of the few teams that modified its steering wheel, while still retaining its characteristic horizontal X shape. With the ban of a number of electronic functions due to the regulations, the wheel was simplified, but, most importantly, its vertical bulk was reduced. The separation of the buttons from the paddles for the management of various programmes (6) was more rational, brought together in the lower central part of the wheel and easily interchangeable if necessary.

2005

McLAREN'S WHEEL

The McLaren steering wheel was practically unchanged and retained a structure that had been introduced in 2002. The strangest feature concerned the elimination of the indications added to the wheel's centre in 2003, now on the right inside the chassis (see the Technical Analyses of 2002 and 2003) on a special sticker that acted as a reminder for the drivers.

2003

2002

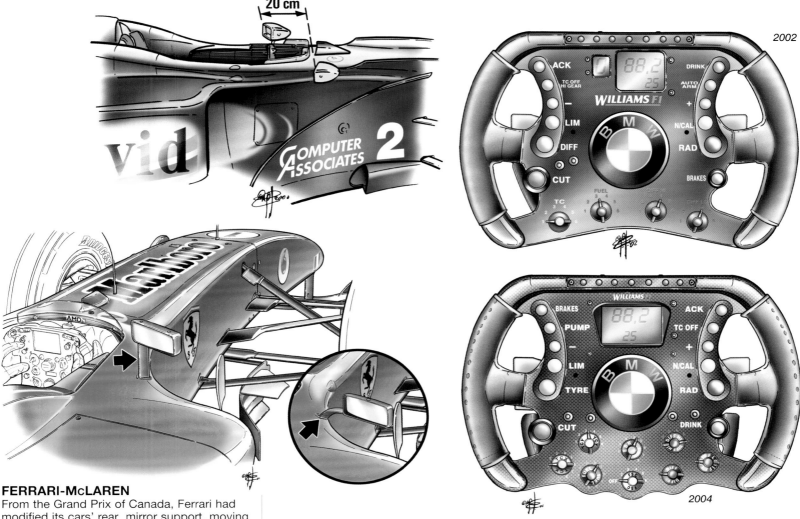

2002

2004

FERRARI-McLAREN

From the Grand Prix of Canada, Ferrari had modified its cars' rear mirror support, moving it higher to achieve a better aerodynamic effect. It was a change used only by Schumacher and unwanted by Barrichello, who kept his mirrors in the original lower position throughout the season. In 2004, McLaren opted for asymmetrically positioned mirrors, with the one on the right about 20 cm farther forward. That was done for the Grand Prix of France to improve driver visibility in the corners that precede the finish straight.

WILLIAMS STEERING WHEEL

The comparison between the Williams BMW steering wheels of 2005 and 2004 shows how much the former was simplified, of different shape down low and had more management paddles – 8 in 2004 and 5 in 2005. Last season's wheel went back to the same shape as that of 2002. The display was bigger, while the lights that indicate gear changes were in a small window above the main display.

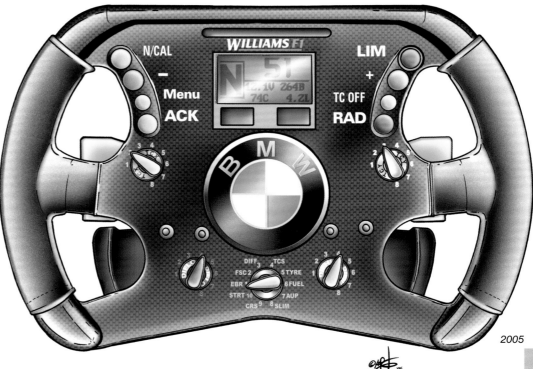

2005

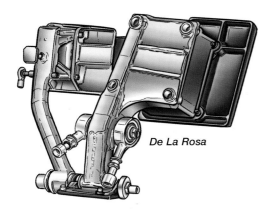

De La Rosa

Raikkonen

McLAREN PEDALS

A comparison between the pedals of Raikkonen and those of De La Rosa, who competed in the Grand Prix of Bahrain in place of the injured Montoya. The Finn used a bigger throttle pedal and larger lateral blocks around the brake pedal. But the Spanish driver had a smaller throttle pedal but with a plate to separate it from the brake. The front view shows Raikkonen's pedals, with the separation plates emphasised between the two elements and the carbon fibre block that reproduces the shape of the ankle, a technique used by many teams.

Ferrari

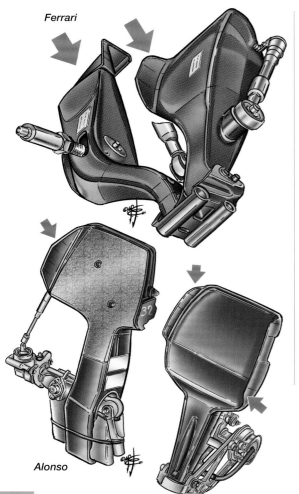

Alonso

THE SCHUMACHER AND ALONSO SEATS

Schumacher retained the unique arrangement of inflated bags of air to improve the driving comfort of his Ferrari's seat, while Alonso used a seat very similar to those of other drivers, with a carbon fibre shell covered in fireproof imitation suede. Both had handles with which they could be extracted from the car in the case of an accident, a system that has been obligatory in F1 since the 2001 season.

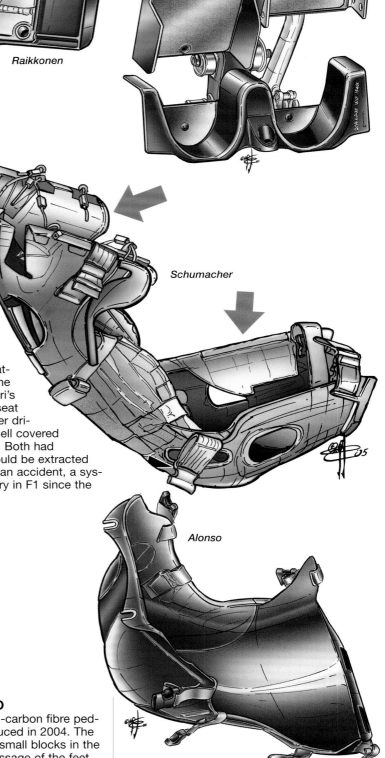

Schumacher

Alonso

FERRARI AND ALONSO

Ferrari and Renault used all-carbon fibre pedals, which Maranello introduced in 2004. The illustration emphasises the small blocks in the material, which stop the passage of the feet from one pedal to another.

TALKING ABOUT SUSPENSIONS

This is another chapter almost entirely dedicated to Renault, which not only won both championships but was also the team that set the trend by introducing new developments in almost all the areas of the car in 2005. The feature that immediately distinguished the new R25 was the V-shaped anchorage of the lower wishbone of the front suspension. It was an open V structure in carbon fibre, which eliminated the negative turbulence originated by the shell without incurring penalisation in terms of weight and rigidity linked to another widespread solution among the teams in recent years: the twin keel. If this new element seemed immediately evident right from the presentation of the R25, the other even more important feature remained jealously hidden for the whole season. It was only before the 2006 Grand Prix of Monaco that it was possible to uncover this secret, which became the subject of open polemics at the Grand Prix of Germany about two months later. The device called a mass damper and was tucked away inside the nose of the car in the area where the latter was not subjected to deformation due to the frontal crash test. Renault had presented this project to the Federation in September 2005, was

subjected to a new crash test, among other things and then used it in the remaining races, in which the R25 seemed more competitive than its rival McLaren. But what did this kind of ballast installed inside the nose of the car consist of? The mass damper was an inertial vibration damper, a nine kilogram mass combined with springs, which therefore generate a vertical oscillation of the system with a frequency that interfered with that created by the tyres in contact with the roughness of the asphalt or kerbs. That is how a notable improvement was obtained in the handling of the tyres, to the advantage of grip and a more constant footprint. The brusque oscillations in jumping

onto the kerbs were damped. The biggest advantage of using this expedient can especially be seen at the front end, where it is possible to push the envelope with much more rigid set-ups, reducing therefore the jump effect by use of the mass damper. According to calculations made by other teams' technicians, the advantage that could be obtained by use of a mass damper was in the order of three tenths of a second per lap.

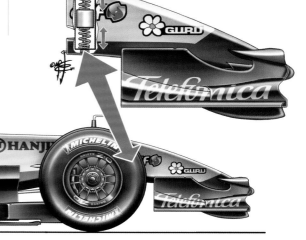

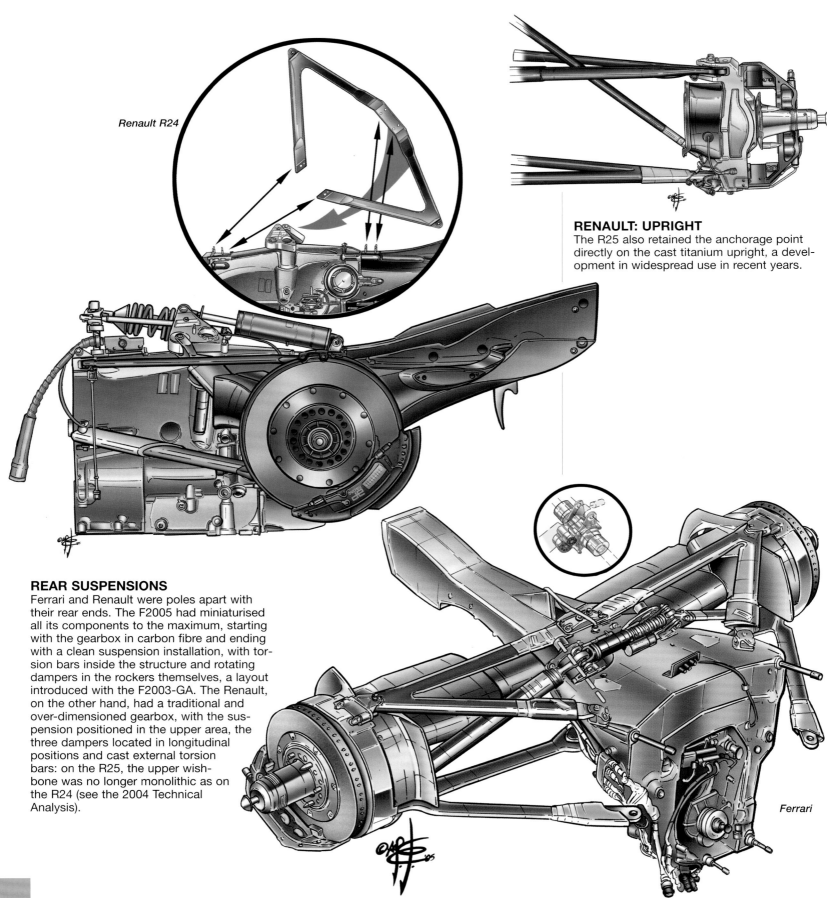

Renault R24

RENAULT: UPRIGHT
The R25 also retained the anchorage point directly on the cast titanium upright, a development in widespread use in recent years.

REAR SUSPENSIONS
Ferrari and Renault were poles apart with their rear ends. The F2005 had miniaturised all its components to the maximum, starting with the gearbox in carbon fibre and ending with a clean suspension installation, with torsion bars inside the structure and rotating dampers in the rockers themselves, a layout introduced with the F2003-GA. The Renault, on the other hand, had a traditional and over-dimensioned gearbox, with the suspension positioned in the upper area, the three dampers located in longitudinal positions and cast external torsion bars: on the R25, the upper wishbone was no longer monolithic as on the R24 (see the 2004 Technical Analysis).

Ferrari

McLAREN-FERRARI

While adopting the torsion bar layout, McLaren located them in a completely different way in relation to the other cars such as Ferrari, for example, where they were threaded from the front part of the chassis in a horizontal manner. On the MP4-20, they were threadable in an oblique sense from the cavity recessed into the chassis, where the suspension rocker was anchored. The position of the dampers (1-2) was, however, very similar to the more traditional one, as shown in the Ferrari layout.

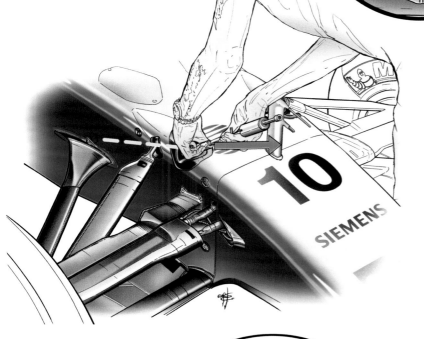

RED BULL

The fashion of fairing the suspension elements with wings sections became widespread during the 2005 season. The team that went farthest in the exploitation of the regulation that allowed a ratio of 3.5 mm between the thickness and width of the wishbones was Red Bull (see the appropriate chapter) with extreme features on both the front and rear ends, all of which was judged legal together with the brake intakes (see the Controversies chapter) in a meeting between the Federation and technical delegates of the various teams.

TOYOTA

Toyota brought in the B version of its TF105 for the last two races of the season. It was a precursor of the team's 2006 car and had new front suspension that was raised to permit a development without the McLaren-type keel. In the comparison, note the new upright with a raised lower wishbone and the new anchorage for the pushrod on this mobile laboratory, which was raced to accumulate experience, gathered with a detachable component so as to find the correct geometry for the suspension itself.

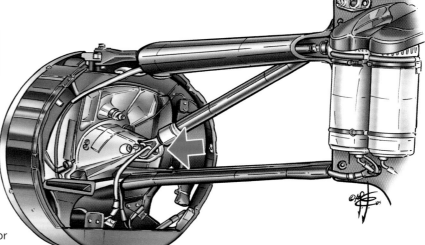

CONTROVERSIES 2005

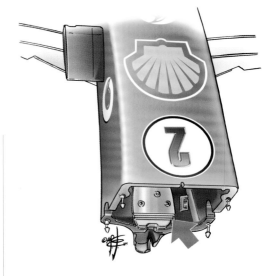

Apart from the championship victories of Renault and Fernando Alonso, which brought an end to Ferrari's five consecutive seasons of dominance, 2005 will be remembered for the Federation's harsh disqualification of BAR for two Grands Prix. This followed scrutineering after the GP of Imola, when a second fuel tank hidden by a separation plate inside the main cell was found on Jenson Button's car. The extra tank had a capacity of 8.9 kg or 11.6 litres and went well beyond the normal nourice content in all the other teams' tanks: its declared purpose was to avoid air bubbles finding their way to the engine. The most serious aspect of the matter was that, after a quick inspection, this nourice was indeed hidden by the separation plate and was operated by its own pump. The heads of the British team defended themselves by referring to the particular needs of the fuel feed system of the 10 cylinder Honda engine, which, in order to function correctly, required a pressure of about 50 bar, moving on from this assumption: to avoid air bubbles reaching the injectors, it was necessary to pass through this nourice of notable capacity. But that line of defence was not accepted by the Federation and nor was the justification for having consumed about 5 kg of oil. So BAR was excluded from the next two races, the Grands Prix of Spain and Monaco for having raced underweight at Imola.

It should be emphasised that, after the happenings at Imola, insistent rumours circulated the pits at Barcelona suggesting that no fewer than another three teams had asked ATL, the supplier of tanks to all F1 teams, to modify to their units.

FERRARI'S BALLASTED NOSE

The need to move considerable weight to the front end to resolve chronic understeer problems linked to the low downforce obtained with the front wings raised by 15 cm in relation to the reference plain, forced the technicians to ballast the central area of the car's nose. The dispute came to a head on the circus's return to Europe, more precisely at the Grand Prix of Europe. The illustration shows the version used by Ferrari, with the ballast positioned in the central part of the nose near the chassis, therefore inside the deformable structure. From the Grand Prix of France, the Federation got into the habit of weighing the noses of the various cars separately to see how far the different teams technicians had gone, maintaining that it was dangerous to worsen the nose situation by adding more weight. A danger that came to light in spectacular fashion in Hungary, where a simple front wing plane that had come off Alonso's Renault caused Coulthard's accident, destroying the front end of his Red Bull. On that occasion, the planes were standard and without any ballast, but the alarm bell had been sounded, bringing about the start of the safety campaign supported by the Federation's chief scrutineer, Charlie Whiting. During the days of the Grand Prix of Belgium, it was learnt that Ralf Schumacher had asked his technicians for a division of the weights that favoured the front of the car in relation to that of Jarno Trulli's TF105, so that Ralf could better control his

Toyota under braking; although the ballast value was rather high in this case, the German driver's car was judged to conform to the regulations.

The debate on this subject continued in the various meetings that took place during the season between the designers of the different teams and the Federation's delegates. The purpose was to fix a maximum weight for the nose planes and end plates for the 2006 season, which should be 14 kg overall. In that way, there would be a value close to the actual overall weight, reducing to almost zero the possibility of adding more ballast. It should be remembered that the nose had to pass the severe crash tests laid down by FIA – front and side impact and tear verifications – while the other nose components such as planes, flaps and end plates had to successfully complete flexing tests.

THE BAR FUEL TANK

This simple illustration shows in red the section hidden by a plate (6) inside the BAR's fuel tank, nourice which contained about 11.6 litres of fuel. (1) The electric pumps sent the petrol to the real (4) from which it was aspirated by a mechanical pump (2) that sent it to the injectors. (3) The fuel was recovered and returned to the tank by the injectors.

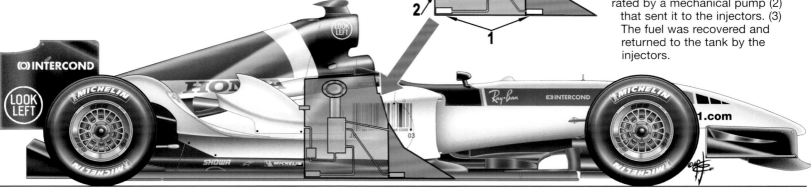

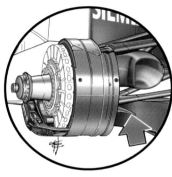

that value of their sum total (steering link and upper wishbone of the front end; upper wishbone, drive shafts and toe-in link at the rear). The small fins on the sides of the open area around the rear wheels shown in the Jordan illustra-tion were also under indictment. Those fea-tures were then judged satisfactory and were, therefore, maintained by right on the cars. Awaiting the outcome of the meeting, Ferrari had removed the little plane-like wing fins above the front brake intakes at Montreal as a precaution, but they went back on the cars from the Grand Prix of France, in line with all the other teams.

CONTROVERSIAL SOLUTIONS

The exaggerated interpretation by many teams of the regulations concerning cooling intakes for the brakes and elements of the suspension was a subject of discussion throughout the 2005 season. The units were actually used as mobile aerodynamic devices and in theory, therefore, were prohibited. From the Grand Prix of Canada and awaiting clarification by the WTG - the working party made up of FIA delegates and technicians of the various teams - small wings masquerad-ing as brake air intakes were banned, like those on the Ferraris at Monaco and a new version on the McLarens at Montreal. The Anglo-German team arrived at Montreal with a new interpretation without the detail shown in the illustration and used until the Grand Prix of Europe: a similar unit on the Toyotas was rejected. Yet the Renault version was accepted because it had small apertures, which were taken up by Toyota in their new example and appeared at Indy. The definitive clarification on the subject came out of the meeting held between the two North Ameri-can races.

In this chapter are illustrated some of the developments that were under investigation: the cooling intake for the Red Bulls' rear brakes of a shape curved upwards towards the rear; the even more accentuated design by McLaren with an entire plane curved upwards and completely unjustified, if one considers reasons linked exclusively to the purpose of cooling.

Also under discussion was the prominent far-ing of the Renaults, which, although it had more neutral planes, had the task of improv-ing the quality of the air flow in that zone and in so doing increase the efficiency of both the low plane of the wing and the diffuser. More uncertain was the case of the narrow cooling intake of the Renault, which was copied for Indy by Toyota and had a slight aperture with an evident aerodynamic function.

Under investigation was the particularly large faring of both the front (see illustration) and rear suspension of Red Bull, which constitut-ed in that sense the most macroscopic exam-ple. The regulation requires a ratio of 3.5 mm between the width and thickness of the sus-pension arms, of a size in this case to obtain

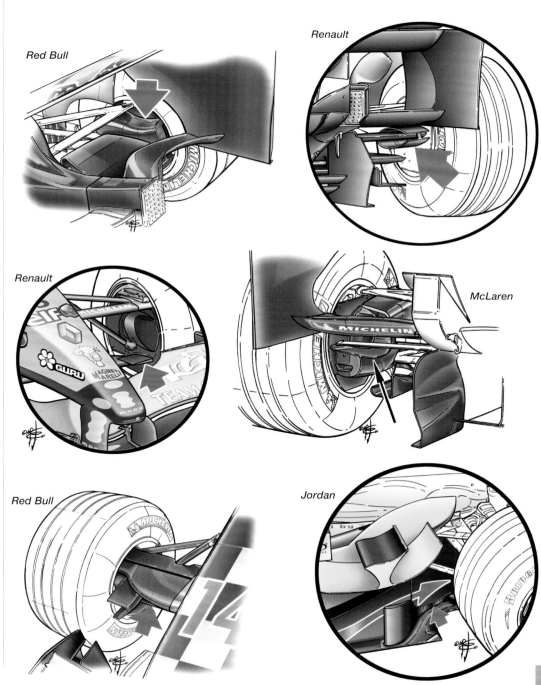

Red Bull

Renault

Renault

McLaren

Red Bull

Jordan

HOW TO BUILD A FORMULA ONE CAR

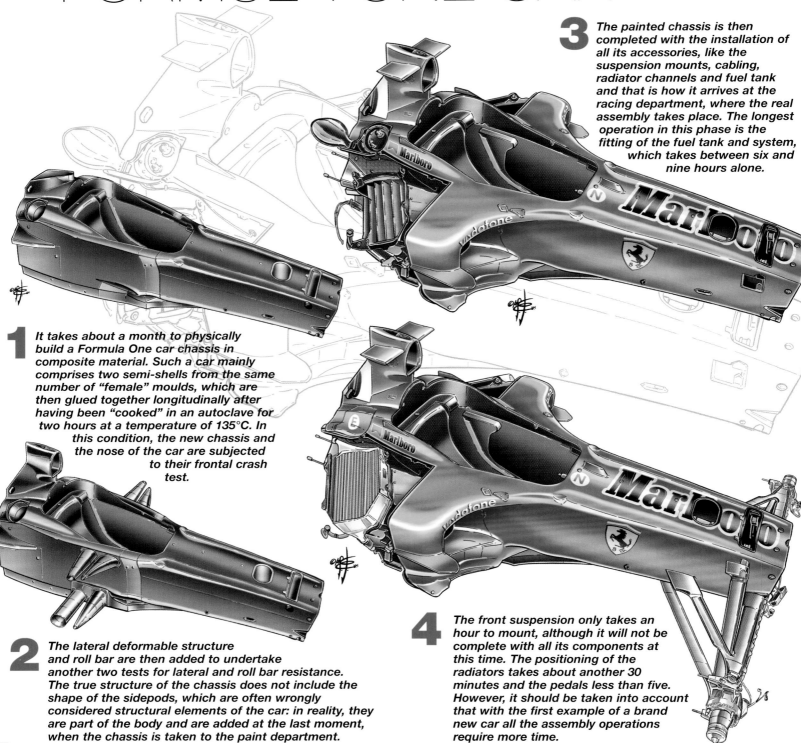

3 *The painted chassis is then completed with the installation of all its accessories, like the suspension mounts, cabling, radiator channels and fuel tank and that is how it arrives at the racing department, where the real assembly takes place. The longest operation in this phase is the fitting of the fuel tank and system, which takes between six and nine hours alone.*

1 *It takes about a month to physically build a Formula One car chassis in composite material. Such a car mainly comprises two semi-shells from the same number of "female" moulds, which are then glued together longitudinally after having been "cooked" in an autoclave for two hours at a temperature of 135°C. In this condition, the new chassis and the nose of the car are subjected to their frontal crash test.*

2 *The lateral deformable structure and roll bar are then added to undertake another two tests for lateral and roll bar resistance. The true structure of the chassis does not include the shape of the sidepods, which are often wrongly considered structural elements of the car: in reality, they are part of the body and are added at the last moment, when the chassis is taken to the paint department.*

4 *The front suspension only takes an hour to mount, although it will not be complete with all its components at this time. The positioning of the radiators takes about another 30 minutes and the pedals less than five. However, it should be taken into account that with the first example of a brand new car all the assembly operations require more time.*

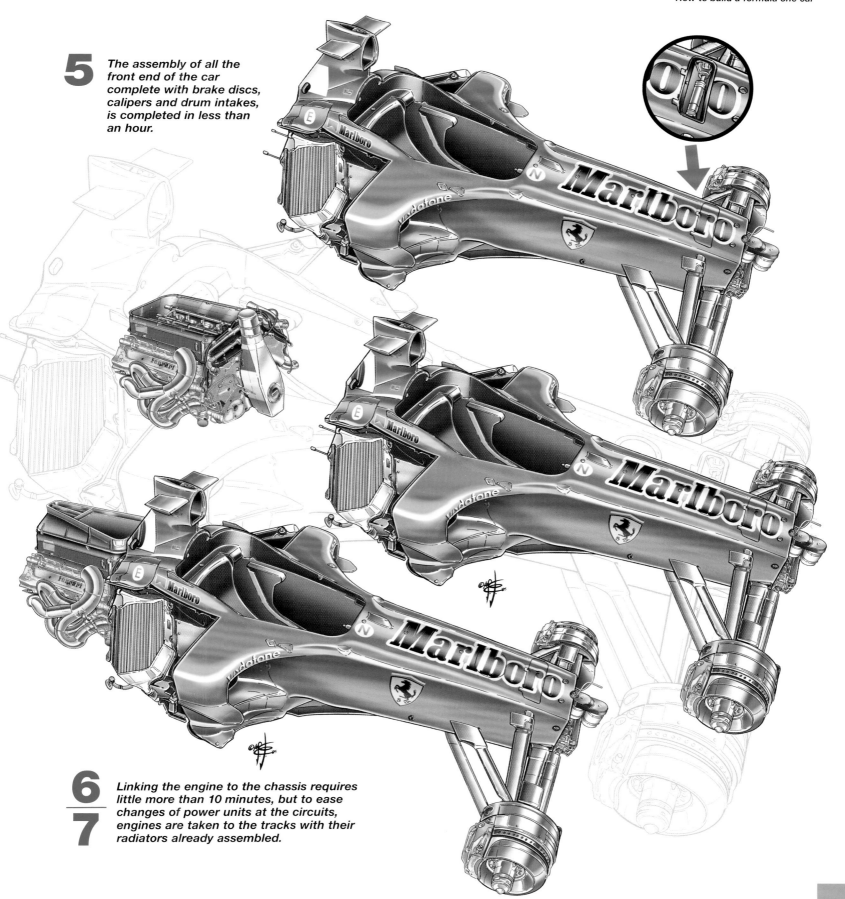

5 The assembly of all the front end of the car complete with brake discs, calipers and drum intakes, is completed in less than an hour.

6/7 Linking the engine to the chassis requires little more than 10 minutes, but to ease changes of power units at the circuits, engines are taken to the tracks with their radiators already assembled.

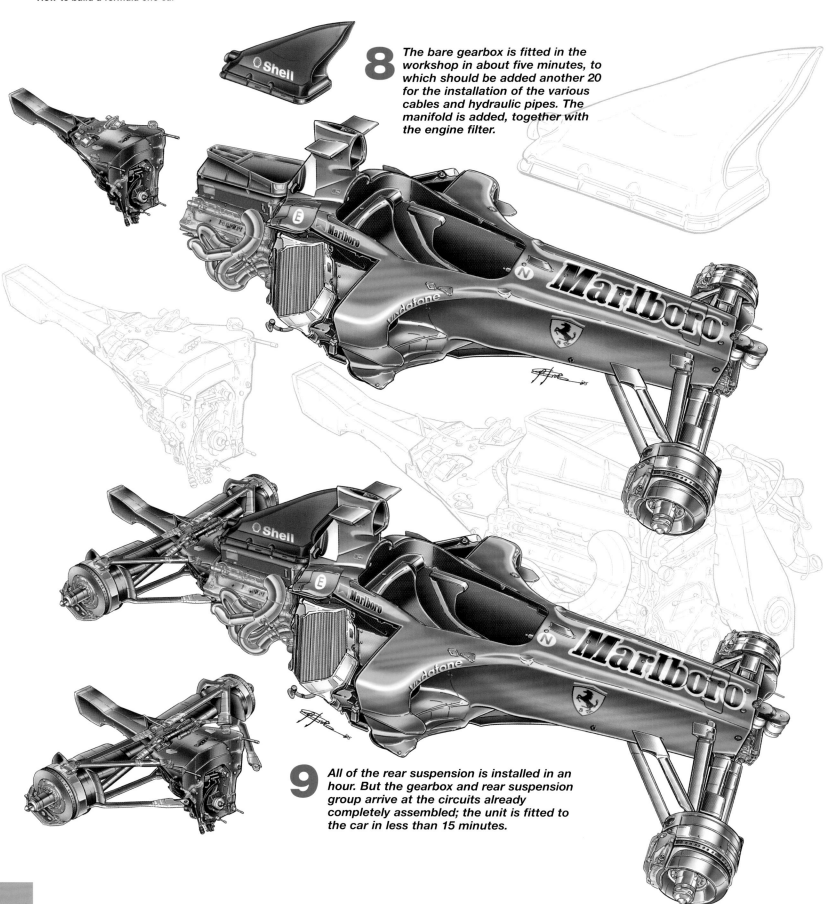

8 The bare gearbox is fitted in the workshop in about five minutes, to which should be added another 20 for the installation of the various cables and hydraulic pipes. The manifold is added, together with the engine filter.

9 All of the rear suspension is installed in an hour. But the gearbox and rear suspension group arrive at the circuits already completely assembled; the unit is fitted to the car in less than 15 minutes.

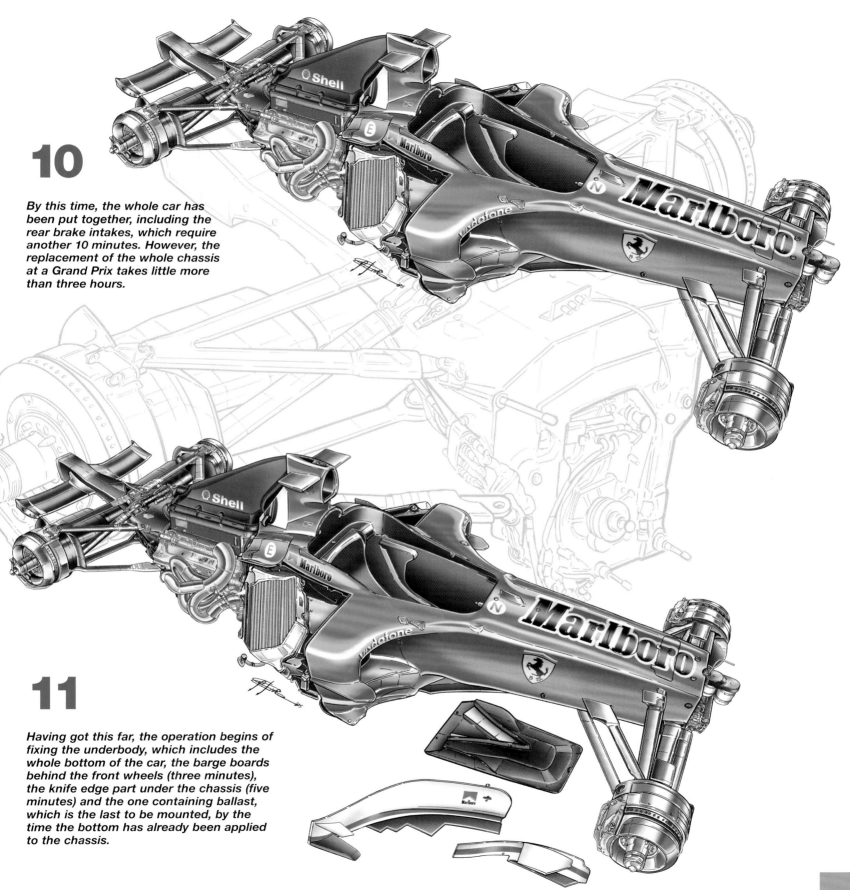

10

By this time, the whole car has been put together, including the rear brake intakes, which require another 10 minutes. However, the replacement of the whole chassis at a Grand Prix takes little more than three hours.

11

Having got this far, the operation begins of fixing the underbody, which includes the whole bottom of the car, the barge boards behind the front wheels (three minutes), the knife edge part under the chassis (five minutes) and the one containing ballast, which is the last to be mounted, by the time the bottom has already been applied to the chassis.

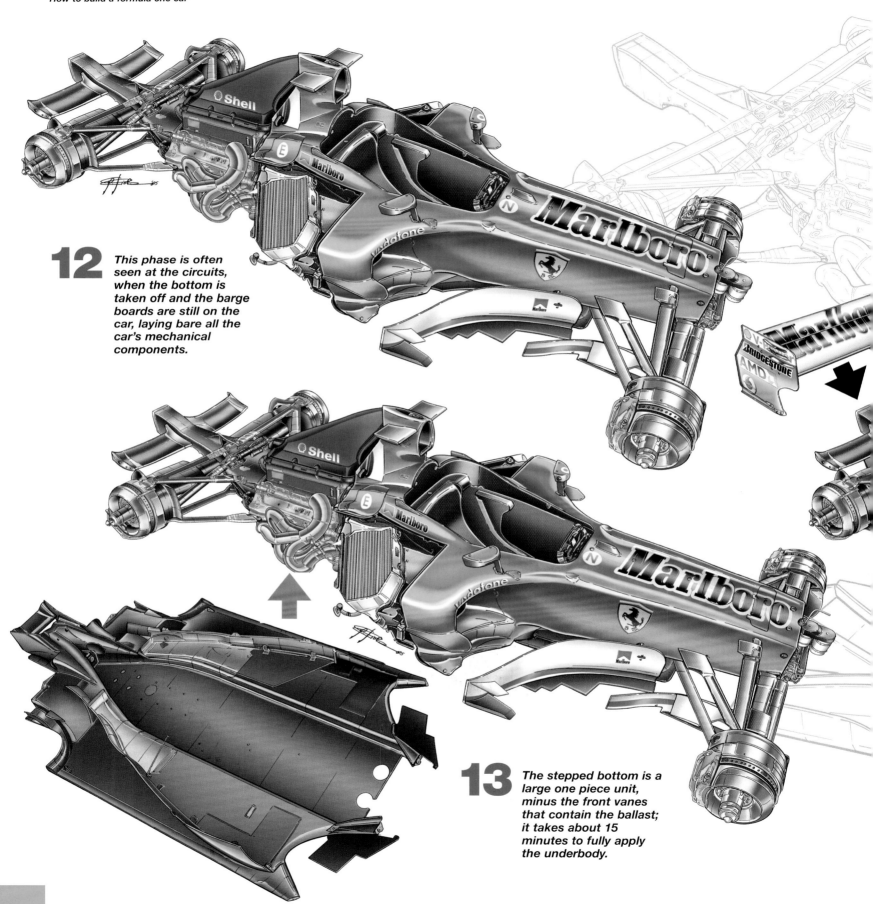

12 This phase is often seen at the circuits, when the bottom is taken off and the barge boards are still on the car, laying bare all the car's mechanical components.

13 The stepped bottom is a large one piece unit, minus the front vanes that contain the ballast; it takes about 15 minutes to fully apply the underbody.

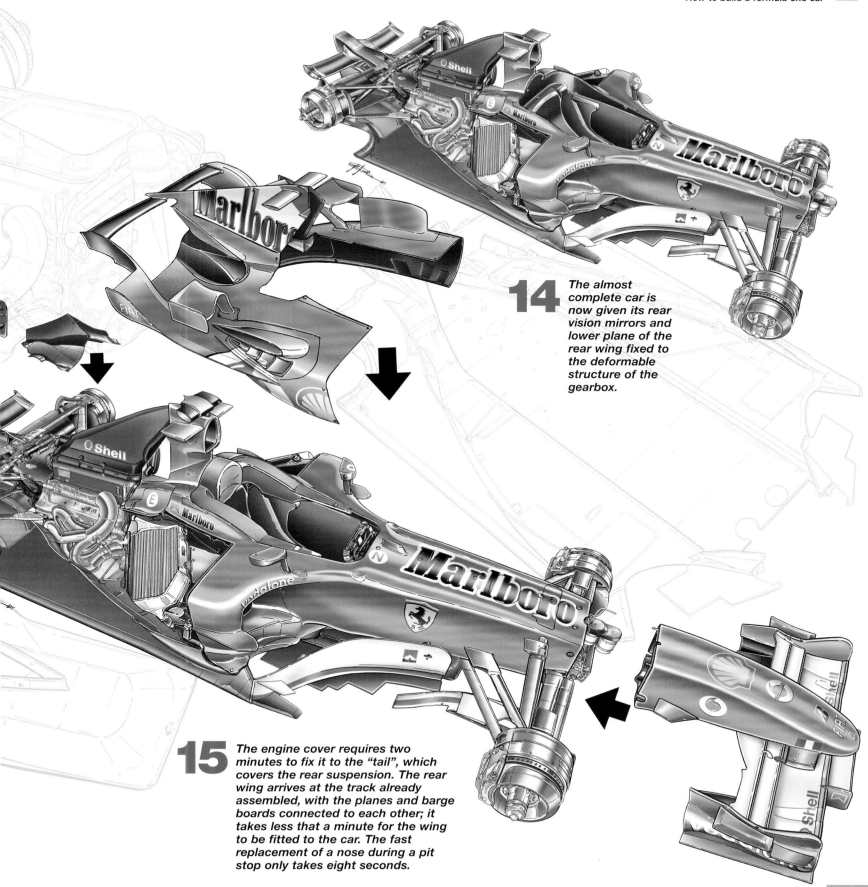

14 The almost complete car is now given its rear vision mirrors and lower plane of the rear wing fixed to the deformable structure of the gearbox.

15 The engine cover requires two minutes to fix it to the "tail", which covers the rear suspension. The rear wing arrives at the track already assembled, with the planes and barge boards connected to each other; it takes less that a minute for the wing to be fitted to the car. The fast replacement of a nose during a pit stop only takes eight seconds.

RENAULT

The R26 designed by Tim Densham was the logical but still radical evolution of the previous year's R25 that was, obviously, adapted to the new regulations, but that did not have the twists of the basic imposition of the 2004 R24's aerodynamics, which were by Bob Bell and supervised by Dino Toso, who became head of Renault's aerodynamics sector after John Iley moved to Ferrari. As did all the other teams, Renault attempted to recover from the serious loss of down-force caused by the new aerodynamic limitations imposed by the Federation for 2005. A loss of about 22% at the time of the car's introduction, which was reduced to around 15% by the first race and halved again by about mid-season. Most of the design work by Pat Symmonds' group, who took over when Mike Gascoyne went to Toyota, was concentrated on three fundamental aspects: a quest for greater mechanical reliability, an attempt to design a car less difficult for the drivers to control on the limit – a defect of the R24 – and

WINGS COMPARISON

In this sequence are the four main evolutions of the R25 seen during the season. The added double flap appeared at Imola in the upper area of the front wing's end plates; at Monaco it was the turn of a further modification of the end plates with the addition of an external gill, together with the introduction of a new engine cover with double flaps in the front and double fins ahead of the rear wheels. New barge boards behind the front wheels made their appearance at Sao Paolo, different fins in front of the rears and a new diffuser. The version used by the team at Monza included wings specifically for that circuit and were not used again.

Renault R24

Renault R25
presentation

Imola

Monaco

San Paolo

research to marry power with reliability in the engine, all of which were achieved in full. The first came from the meticulous task of checking the quality control unit, which was established at Enstone in an effort to avoid problems like the one that afflicted Giancarlo Fisichella in Canada, where he was stopped by a hydraulic fault the design of which had remained that of 2004, and that got past quality control even with that constructional defect. The second objective was achieved by trying to arrive at a correct equilibrium between aerodynamic solutions and track set-ups in order to have a car with the more neutral reactions on the circuit. Renault was, in fact, one of the teams that went farthest down the road in its search for aerodynamic efficiency in its 2005 car, without having to pursue the load values obtained during the previous season, before the substantial cuts in aerodynamics brought in by FIA. The engine was in its second year, its architecture reduced from 111° to just 72° and the only one in F1 without a cylinder bank angle of 90°. Work was directed by Rob White and concentrated on the search for more power, while conceding nothing in terms of reliability. In direct comparison with McLaren,

Renault dominated in the area of general reliability, due to a constructional philosophy that attempted to zero the risk/performance relationship. An approach that was an inversion of tendency in relation to what was the constructional philosophy of the same working party to which Rory Byrne belonged in the days of Benetton.
At first glance, the R25 did not seem to have strayed much from the previous year's car: it retained the fundamental parameters of the aerodynamics, wheelbase and weight distribution, developed to favour the front end, unlike the direction taken by its immediate rivals, McLaren. As far as weight distribution is concerned, it should be said that, of the top teams, Renault were, perhaps, able to take on the least amount of ballast as a result of the greater weight of the engine-gearbox group. As Symmonds pointed out, the great physical bulk and, therefore, weight of the 'box was an intentional factor in order to achieve superior rigidity of the entire rear end. The gearbox was not designed simply as a container of gears and a key support for the suspension mounts, but rather as an element that had to support all the downforce at the rear end and all the stress the car

underwent on the track. It is in that light that the two carbon fibre stiffeners that link the gearbox to the chassis should be seen, and which had already appeared on the R23 in 2003. Renault and McLaren were the only teams to drop the classic concepts of both the mono-keel and the more innovative twin keel, which had already been seen on the McLaren MP4-19. However, the R25 adopted a V-shaped keel, a new development close to Pat Symmonds' heart, which he calls the most interesting facet of the car. In effect, this feature provided all the aerodynamic advantages of the twin keel, but without running into trouble with the inevitable handicap of torsional rigidity and weight as far as the lower wishbone mounts are concerned, remaining monolithic on the R25. Compared to the McLaren, the Renault was down on performance in qualifying and, especially with full tanks, it produced greater rear tyre wear, probably due to the heavier weight on the back axle. A problem that came to light macroscopically at the Grand Prix of Monaco, which the team did not win because its car

took on too much fuel, producing negative consequences as far as Michelin tyre yield went. But the French covers performed better during the race, often also linked to the best strategies set in motion. A more sophisticated gearbox worked in the McLaren MP4-20's favour and enabled the team to zero dead time during changes, while lightening starts were the advantage of the R25, as was seen at the Grand Prix of Turkey. This, despite the further limitations imposed by the Federation during the winter break in relation to electronic support devices for starting: the all-automatic start procedure has been banned since the 2004 season, having been introduced by ex-Nissan technician Naoki Tokunaga.
The evolution of the car sparked off continual updates, especially to the aerodynamics, with numerous micro-developments concentrated on the front wing. Renault brought in interesting new ideas in this area, like the positioning of a raised mini-flap on the front wing, which appeared at Imola. This enabled the team to increase the front end load, while also positively

SIDEPODS AND ENGINE COVER
One of the Renault's strong points was its aerodynamics, which recaptured the concepts expressed on the R24, starting with the large chimneys and including "shark shoal" air vents (3), which characterised this car. The exhaust terminals (1) were completely new and were lower, without the large chimneys. The little flaps were dif-

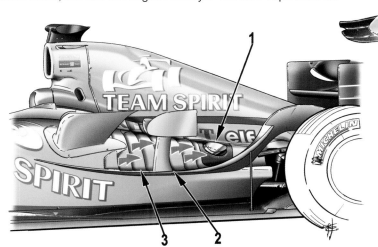

ferent, as they now had central support (2). The Coke bottle shape of the rear part of the car was even more accentuated and the engine cover was much lower.

influencing the airflow towards the car's body without damaging rear end downforce, as usually happens in the presence of a major incidence of flap at the front. It was only on the Saturday morning at Monaco that a further sophistication of the front wing end plates was revealed - a new lateral gill on the outside: a feature never previously seen, which made the air flow in that area more energetic so as to increase the efficiency of the principal plane. At the same time, a careful study was carried out on the method of production and painting the additional flap above the main unit, to better differentiate the speed of the air between the upper and lower planes. The small devices in the upper chassis were removed in Spain, having been retained until the Grand Prix of France: they worked in symbiosis with the double flap to straighten the flow of air towards the central and rear areas of the car. The final aerodynamic evolution appeared in Brazil where the rear wing, diffuser plane, engine cover and barge boards behind the front wheels were modified, as was the rear suspension. Five evolutions of the engine were developed, with the final E version being introduced for the last race of the season in China.

STIFFENING

The two links in carbon fibre that strengthened the whole central-rear area of the R25 were retained: they connected the initial area of the gearbox with the chassis, ensuring better torsional rigidity.

THE V-SHAPED KEEL

The most important new aspect of the R25 was the abandonment of the classic shell that anchored the lower wishbone of the suspension for a new V-shaped carbon fibre structure (1), completely permeable and with an extremely favourable torsional/weight stiffness ratio, compared to the twin keel. Note the "soft spoon" feature (2) of the principal plane, which then raised itself upwards (3) to connect with the end plates.

GEARBOX

The R25 had a titanium gearbox of extremely generous dimensions, which was similar to that of the R24. The rear suspension layout was also unchanged, with its dampers placed horizontally in the upper area. The torsion bars were attached directly to the inside of the rockers. In the illustration of the assembled gearbox, note the two stiffeners in carbon fibre that link with the chassis to provide greater rear end rigidity.

FRONT WING

Renault did not aim for high load values at the front end so as not to have to adopt wings of anomalous or pronounced shape, always critical in relation to the variations in the car's height from the ground. It was not by chance that the principal plane was "soft spoon" shaped and without substantial overhang: the height from the ground in the end plate area was greater in relation to the progression of the plane.

IMOLA

A new raised flap in relation to the traditional ones was introduced at Imola to load the front end as much as possible without needing substantial incidence, but more than anything else to improve the flow of air towards the central and rear zones of the car and partially straighten the flow exiting the front wing.

THE "DOLPHIN'S NOSE"

This divergence in the lower area of the R25 called the dolphin's nose interested everybody at Sepang, because it broke on Fisichella's car. As well as the purely aerodynamic function of sending the air flow to the lower area of the car, it contained internal ballast.

DIFFUSER

There were new diffusers for the Renault, with two external mini-channels (2) in the area of the lateral ones. Note the large faring of the wing plane (1) in the zone permitted by the regulations. Like many other teams, in practice Renault used a laser reader (3) to check their cars' height from the ground.

THE "EARS" OF BARCELONA

The R25 arrived at Barcelona with these small aerodynamic ear-like devices in the upper area of the chassis. They were inspired by the analogous units used the previous year by Williams and this year by Toyota to better balance the cars by directing the air flow towards their rear. They stayed on the R25 until the Grand Prix of France, the race at which they also appeared on the Williams.

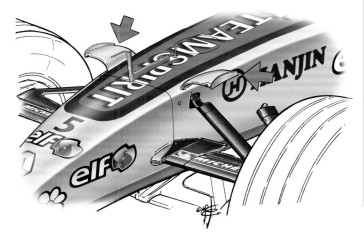

IMOLA

The new double flap brought in by Renault at Imola was copied during the season by many other teams. This view shows how the incidence was minimal and how its plane is amply curled in order to improve the air flow towards the central wall of the car, avoiding a brusque detachment of the fluid vein.

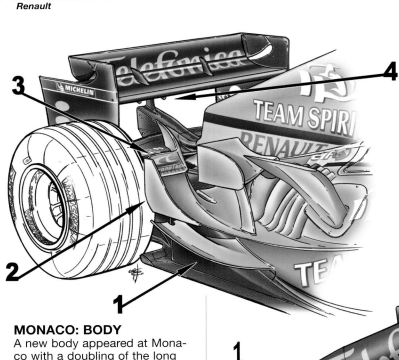

MONACO: BODY

A new body appeared at Monaco with a doubling of the long fins in front of the rear wheels, and with flaps in the upper area (2), also delimited by a larger vertical vane (3).

MONTREAL: REAR WING

For a medium-fast track like Montreal, the R25 had a new rear wing with its flap reduced in height (1) and combined with a plane that had gone back to having a raised peripheral zone near the end plates, compared to its central area (2).

WINGLET

A small winglet above the rear light, an idea first introduced by Williams in Australia, appeared on the R25 as part of Renault's search for a few kilograms more downforce for the rear end. The team also took an important new development to Monaco concerning the end plates, which had been given an external mini-channel with a rear blow so as to increase the efficiency of the usable surface of the main plane, a new feature which is also illustrated in the aerodynamics chapter.

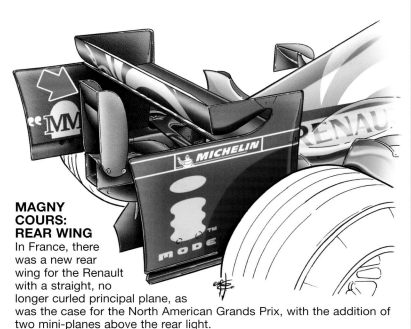

MAGNY COURS: REAR WING

In France, there was a new rear wing for the Renault with a straight, no longer curled principal plane, as was the case for the North American Grands Prix, with the addition of two mini-planes above the rear light.

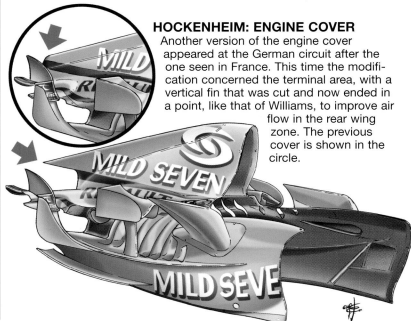

HOCKENHEIM: ENGINE COVER

Another version of the engine cover appeared at the German circuit after the one seen in France. This time the modification concerned the terminal area, with a vertical fin that was cut and now ended in a point, like that of Williams, to improve air flow in the rear wing zone. The previous cover is shown in the circle.

WING: SEEN FROM BELOW

From this low angle, it is easier to understand how the main plane remained unchanged at Monza, while the flap was reduced in the chord. Note the lateral mini-channels in the end plate of the wing, which were also retained on the version used at Monza.

MONZA: FRONT WING

The aerodynamic configuration devised for Monza led to the elimination of the front end flap connected to the Renault's end plates, which were very low in the front and inclined inwards. The team's two drivers used flaps of different sizes, even if the two had much more reduced chords than usual, as can be seen in both the side and overhead views.

SPA-FRANCORCHAMPS: FRONT WING

Renault kept the front wing, first seen at Monza, with its low end plates and without the double flap, which, however, reappeared at the following race in Brazil. Four different flaps were available, obviously fitted with greater incidence in relation to those at Monza. Note the difference in colour created by the presence of the Kevlar skin, which was obligatory this season to avoid the scattering of debris caused by aerodynamic components most subject to breakage in the case of an accident.

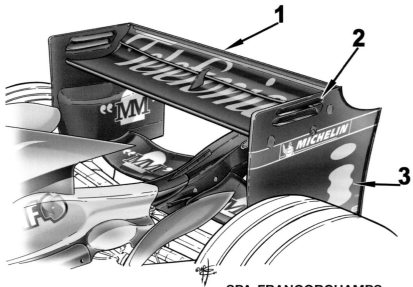

SPA-FRANCORCHAMPS: REAR WING

Renault brought to Spa a rear wing that was new in all its components, one that retained almost the same end plates as those of Monza, but with an additional two horizontal apertures (2) at the top and the elimination of the vertical one (3), which was on the Monza end plate. Both the wing's planes were new and had a straight flap (1).

SUPPLEMENTARY OIL RESERVOIR

As was the case at Sepang and Indianapolis, Renault installed an additional small oil reservoir above the car's manifold for the Belgian Grand Prix to deal with the expected increased consumption of liquid due to the very high revolutions on each lap of the Spa circuit.

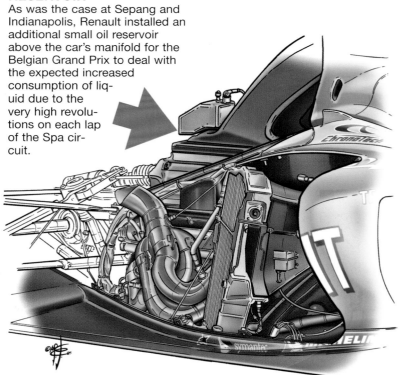

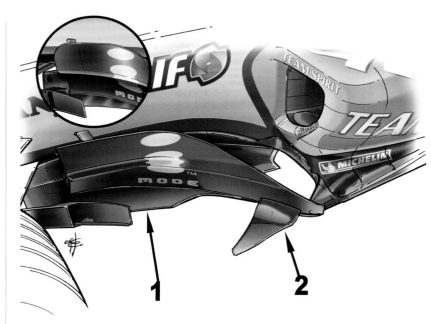

SAO PAOLO: BARGE BOARDS BEHIND THE FRONT WHEELS

There was a new aerodynamic package for Renault in Brazil, starting with the barge boards behind the front wheels. The biggest difference was the more angular shape high up on their leading edge, as can be seen by comparing them with the old version in the circle. They were also much more concave towards the inside low down, and it was for this reason that the knife-edge zone (1) was wider. The shape of the fin in front of the sidepods (2) was also different and first appeared the previous year at Monaco: it was always used on the Renault, even if in differing ways.

SAO PAOLO: ENGINE COVER

The engine cover was also modified: it was slightly lower in the terminal area and recognisable from those used at Monza and Spa by the return of the gills at the end of the fin in front of the rear wheels, as indicated by the red arrow.

SAO PAOLO: NEW DIFFUSER

The stepped bottom was completely revised in both the front linkage area with the rest of the car and the rear end with the diffuser planes. This grill (1), which was added to the central part of the faring, hid the laser reader that checked the height of the car from the ground, a device also used during the race. The details of the lateral channels (2-3) were new and worked together with the wide faring of the lower wishbone and the toe-in link to achieve the maximum diffusion of air from the lower area of the lateral channels.

SUZUKA: REAR SUSPENSION

For the last two races of the season, Renault modified the rear suspension of its cars, placing the anchorage points of the upper wishbone towards the outside in order to have a different geometry and better traction, as shown in the circle.

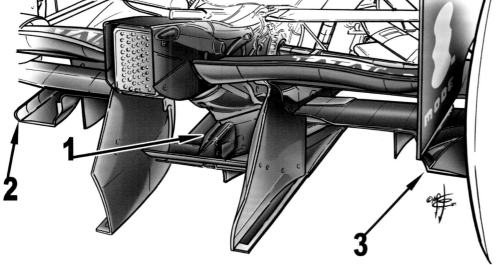

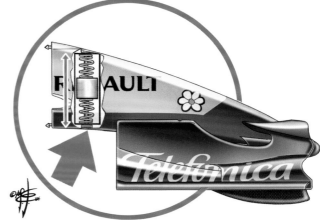

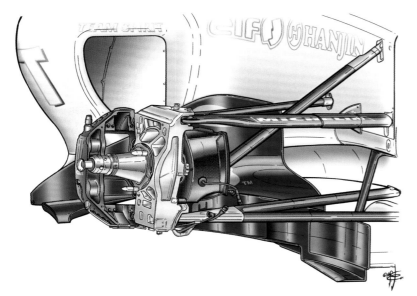

UPRIGHT

The cast titanium upright of the R25, with the pushrod mounts sunken directly into it and no longer into the lower wishbone, which remained the monolithic type due to the adoption of the V-shaped keel. Note that Renault retained its standard cooling inlets, without ever using the drums introduced by Ferrari in 2002 and which were later adopted by almost all the cars.

MASS DAMPER

It was only at the 2006 Grand Prix of Monaco that Renault's secret was discovered and was one that gave the team's cars an advantage from as early as the latter part of the 2005 season. It was a device known as the mass damper, which comprised about 9 kg of ballast mounted on two springs, which limited the frequent vibration generated by the tyres in contact with the ground. The feature was banned by the Federation from the 2006 Grand Prix of Germany.

McLAREN

McLaren MP4-19

McLaren MP4-20
presentation

Sepang

San Paolo

Without doubt, the McLaren MP4-20 was the most beautiful and interesting car of recent years, born from the basis of the two previous projects, which were most decidedly extreme. The starting point was the B version of the MP4-19, which made its debut at the 2004 Grand Prix of France. An extreme car in the best tradition of the those that have emanated from Adrian Newey's drawing board, marked by almost obsessive aerodynamic research and attention to detail. The "Viking horns" were totally new and were extreme examples of those that, in general, are simple mini-planes in the area behind the engine air intake. That development produced a saving in terms of rear wing incidence and at the same time improved the car's aerodynamic efficiency. But reliability was lacking in the battle with arch-rival Renault, especially as far as the Mercedes-Benz engine was concerned. The power unit often forced Raikkonen into incredible drives to climb back up the field, having had to change his 10-cylinder during practice and, as a result, made to start 10 places further back on the grid than the position he achieved in qualifying. Because a car must not only be fast but must also be able to finish a race, Renault in that sense deservedly prevailed over McLaren, a car that was, nevertheless, a technological gem. McLaren had two great advantages: speed in changing gear due to the quick shift gearbox, and a lower tyre wear rate during the race, which often enabled them to select the more extreme Michelins that were also capable of better performance. The tyre factor constituted a performance handicap on the single qualifying lap early in the season, but opportune modifications of the suspension and weight distribution introduced at Imola resolved the problem. As far as weight distribution is concerned, McLaren had the greatest concentration at the front end at about 48%: during the season, the team worked hard to modify the suspension of the car to be driven by Montoya, whose driving style did not align with the basic characteristics of the MP4-20. Development work was continuous and was based on the extreme refinement of every small detail, already being exceptionally well equilibrated and easy to set up for the characteristics of each circuit. Only two different diffuser planes were used during the entire season, while the team worked a great deal on the front wing, which underwent constant development. It is interesting to note the different alignment between the front wing end plate and the front wheels. Newey most certainly sacrificed almost all of the width permitted by the regulations (140 cm) to move the end plates

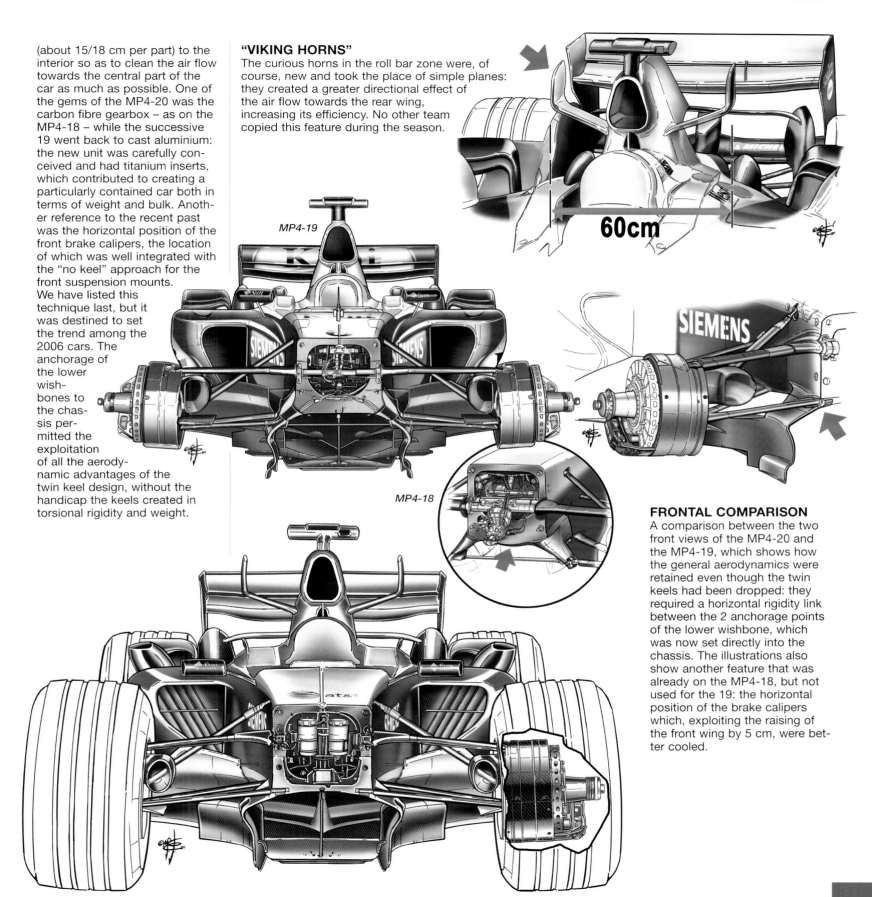

(about 15/18 cm per part) to the interior so as to clean the air flow towards the central part of the car as much as possible. One of the gems of the MP4-20 was the carbon fibre gearbox – as on the MP4-18 – while the successive 19 went back to cast aluminium: the new unit was carefully conceived and had titanium inserts, which contributed to creating a particularly contained car both in terms of weight and bulk. Another reference to the recent past was the horizontal position of the front brake calipers, the location of which was well integrated with the "no keel" approach for the front suspension mounts. We have listed this technique last, but it was destined to set the trend among the 2006 cars. The anchorage of the lower wishbones to the chassis permitted the exploitation of all the aerodynamic advantages of the twin keel design, without the handicap the keels created in torsional rigidity and weight.

"VIKING HORNS"
The curious horns in the roll bar zone were, of course, new and took the place of simple planes: they created a greater directional effect of the air flow towards the rear wing, increasing its efficiency. No other team copied this feature during the season.

60cm

MP4-19

MP4-18

SIEMENS

FRONTAL COMPARISON
A comparison between the two front views of the MP4-20 and the MP4-19, which shows how the general aerodynamics were retained even though the twin keels had been dropped: they required a horizontal rigidity link between the 2 anchorage points of the lower wishbone, which was now set directly into the chassis. The illustrations also show another feature that was already on the MP4-18, but not used for the 19: the horizontal position of the brake calipers which, exploiting the raising of the front wing by 5 cm, were better cooled.

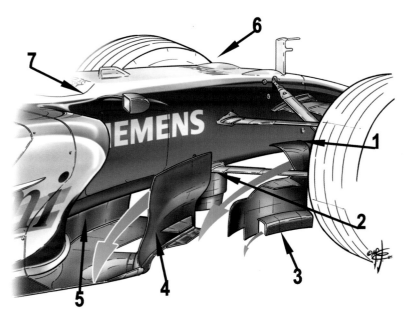

NOSE

The nose constitutes an amalgam of solutions inspired by both the MP4-19B and the MP4-18: the flat, wide central part of the 2004 car's nose was only used at Monza, where it was combined with the front wing first seen on the 2003 car, with large, heavily spooned upper deck flaps.

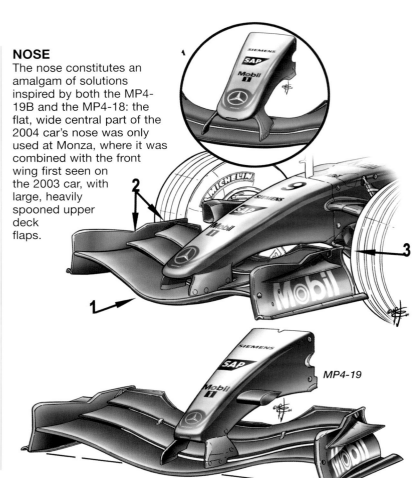

MP4-19

BARGE BOARDS

All the aerodynamics of the MP4-20 were based on development concepts already expressed by the MP4-19B. Even without the twin keel, the end plates began (1) in the chassis mount zone and they split into two elements (3-4) behind the front wheels. The lower wishbone was completely set into the chassis (3). Note the large divergence (5) in the area under the driver's legs. The upper area of the chassis had small protuberances (6) so that there could be a greater inclination of the pushrod, while the steering wheel area was raised and stepped (7), as on the MP4-19B.

HORIZONTAL BRAKES

The MP4-20 went back to using horizontal brake calipers in order to lower the centre of gravity of the unsuspended mass. Note the grooved Carbon Industry discs used by Raikkonen. The different anchorages of the brake calipers can be seen in the comparison with the uprights, as well as the diverse fairing inside the air intake that cools the discs themselves.

MP4-19B

REAR BRAKE INTAKE

The intake was retained that wrapped itself around the discs to avoid heat interfering with tyre pressures. The main change was the different fairing of the upright, which was now free in the upper part of the MP4-20.

MIDDLE WING

Before the Grand Prix of Imola, the mount with the engine cover of the plane fixed above the rear axle was made more rigid.

BARCELONA

The McLaren had a new rear wing, with a main plane that once again took up the concept already seen the previous year of the portion near the end plates raised (2), as shown in yellow. The end plates of the flaps above the cut sidepods remained (1) and were "appreciated" at Imola.

IMOLA

A new rear wing and diffuser also for McLaren: on the MP4-20 two mini-planes appeared on the sides of the rear lights. The lateral channels plane and the central tunnel of the diffuser were different.

MANIFOLD

The manifold was very small and low, inspired by that of the MP4-19 and was integrated with the shape of the roll bar.

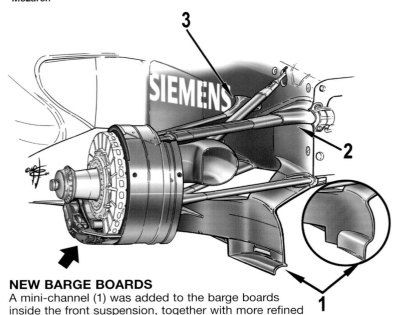

NEW BARGE BOARDS
A mini-channel (1) was added to the barge boards inside the front suspension, together with more refined fairing (2-3) for the upper wishbone mounts.

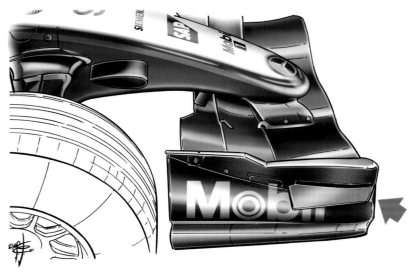

MONTREAL: FRONT WING
A new front wing for McLaren, with two different flaps and a new end plate, which had a much shorter external fin than those used up until that time.

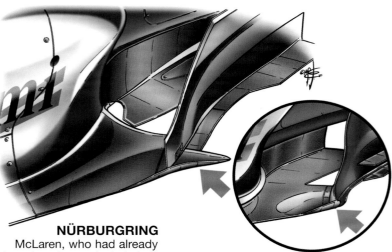

NÜRBURGRING
McLaren, who had already introduced a particularly knife edge portion down low on the MP4-19B at the 2004 Grand Prix of France, followed the fashion created by BAR and then taken up by Williams, Ferrari and Minardi, by adopting a small extension in front of the flat part of the knife edge of both the sidepods on Raikkonen's car and only on the right side of Montoya's. It was a surprise move on the Saturday for qualifying on both cars: the components arrived by aircraft at Cologne at 11.30 am and were flown to the circuit by helicopter.

MP4-19B

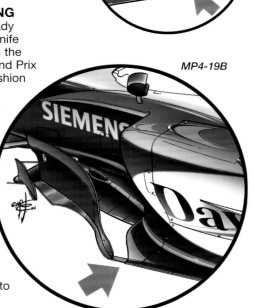

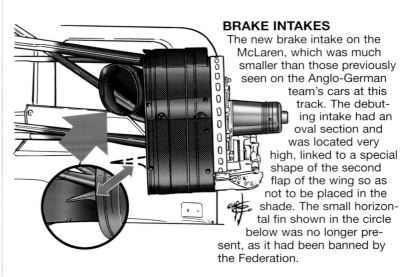

BRAKE INTAKES
The new brake intake on the McLaren, which was much smaller than those previously seen on the Anglo-German team's cars at this track. The debuting intake had an oval section and was located very high, linked to a special shape of the second flap of the wing so as not to be placed in the shade. The small horizontal fin shown in the circle below was no longer present, as it had been banned by the Federation.

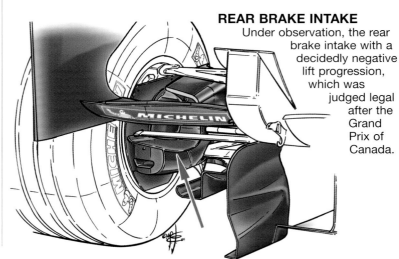

REAR BRAKE INTAKE
Under observation, the rear brake intake with a decidedly negative lift progression, which was judged legal after the Grand Prix of Canada.

HOCKENHEIM

A new front wing appeared in Germany, which partially repeated the end plates introduced in Canada (1) and had very short external fins. The external portion of the end plates (2) was increased in relation to the one used by Wurz, which had the old nose. Experiments were carried out on variations of the ratio between the width of the planes and the external section of the end plates, which were subjected to notable changes with the increase in the front wing group's height from the ground. The planes with two flaps with very thin planes (3) were also new.

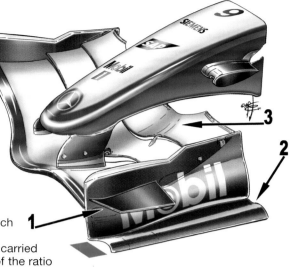

ISTANBUL

Many races earlier, McLaren optimised its cooling with chimneys of three different dimensions, combined with vents in the upper area of the sidepods. The illustration shows the version designed for maximum heat dissipation.

BUDAPEST

A comparison between the new front end plates of the McLaren (below) with a more internal alignment in relation to the tyres so that the external portion became broader (2) and the width of the planes was slightly reduced by 3/4 cm each. According to the reasons provided by the team, this was a solution required to rectify the problem of rubber particles being deposited onto the terminal part of the end plates and reduces their efficiency. The small external fin (2) was different: it was wider and shorter – neutral, without inclination. The difference also concerned the small lip on the inside, which was reduced in relation to the standard version.

HOCKENHEIM

The new rear wing, with end plates inspired by those of Toyota, was not used in qualifying, just on the Friday by both drivers. The unit had three slots in the upper area to recuperate downforce.

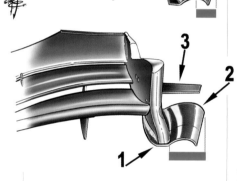

REAR WING

McLaren was the team that used a rear wing with the bigger chord, linked together with the end plates at the start of the season without Toyota-type gills.

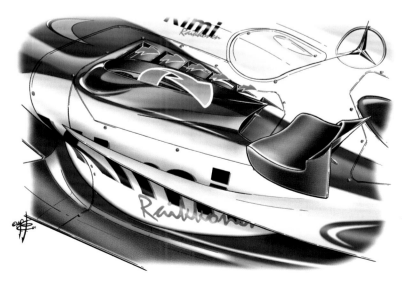

VERTICAL END PLATES

McLaren used these Jaguar-type vertical end plates in front of the rear wheels throughout the season: their task was to better channel the air towards the diffuser plane.

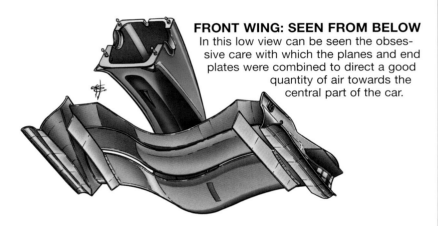

FRONT WING: SEEN FROM BELOW

In this low view can be seen the obsessive care with which the planes and end plates were combined to direct a good quantity of air towards the central part of the car.

TORSION BARS

The torsion bars were set into the suspension rocker, the chassis mount of which was raised to achieve better geometry of the suspension, also in consideration of the elimination of the twin keel.

MONZA

Monza was once again the season's only race at which the classic planes in the shape of "horns" behind the roll bar were not used: they reappeared from the Grand Prix of Belgium.

MONZA

A front wing was used at Monza with just two planes: the chord was not much reduced but mounted, as can be seen in the detail, with very little incidence.

CHASSIS

The separation of the large lateral barge boards enables us to see how concave was the shape of the MP4-20's chassis: note, in particular, the extension of the sidepods inclined forwards, which corresponds to the analogous extension introduced at the Nürburgring.

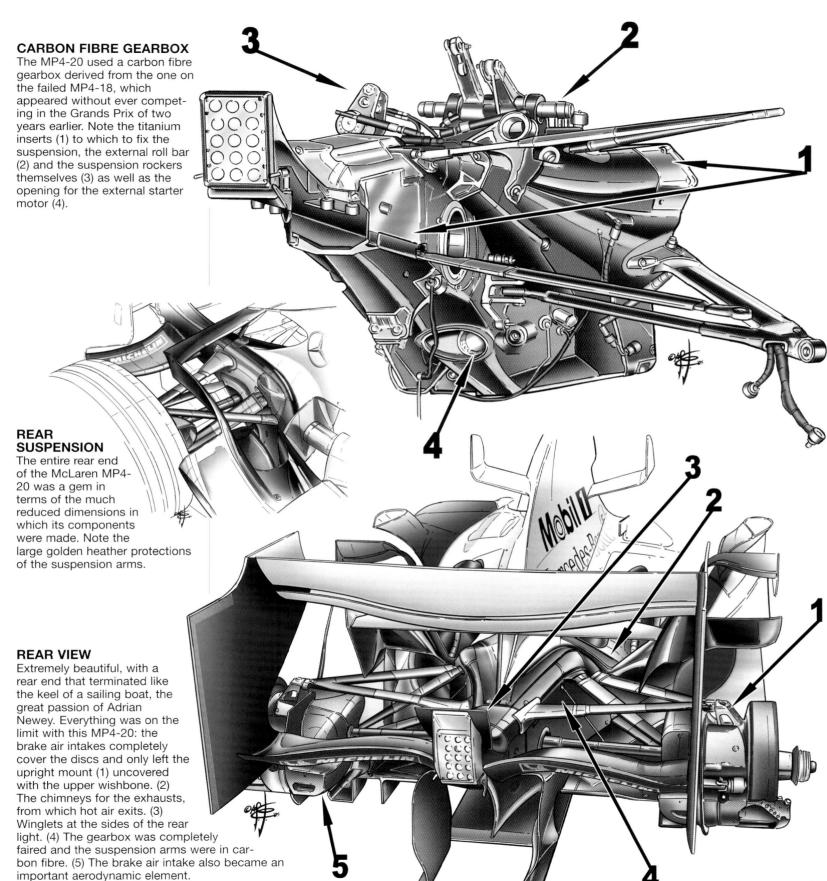

CARBON FIBRE GEARBOX

The MP4-20 used a carbon fibre gearbox derived from the one on the failed MP4-18, which appeared without ever competing in the Grands Prix of two years earlier. Note the titanium inserts (1) to which to fix the suspension, the external roll bar (2) and the suspension rockers themselves (3) as well as the opening for the external starter motor (4).

REAR SUSPENSION

The entire rear end of the McLaren MP4-20 was a gem in terms of the much reduced dimensions in which its components were made. Note the large golden heather protections of the suspension arms.

REAR VIEW

Extremely beautiful, with a rear end that terminated like the keel of a sailing boat, the great passion of Adrian Newey. Everything was on the limit with this MP4-20: the brake air intakes completely cover the discs and only left the upright mount (1) uncovered with the upper wishbone. (2) The chimneys for the exhausts, from which hot air exits. (3) Winglets at the sides of the rear light. (4) The gearbox was completely faired and the suspension arms were in carbon fibre. (5) The brake air intake also became an important aerodynamic element.

FERRARI

CONSTRUCTORS' CLASSIFICATION			
	2004	2005	
Position	1°	3°	-2 ▼
Points	262	100	-162 ▼

Ferrari F2004

Ferrari F2004M

Ferrari F2005

Ferrari F2005
Brasil

It was to be expected that, sooner or later, Ferrari's technical supremacy would come to an end. After all, its run of success started by winning the 1999 Constructors' Championship after which it won another six such titles: and Michael Schumacher made the drivers' championship his for five successive years. But nobody could possibly have guessed the Prancing Horse would experience such a negative season in 2005. The complex regulation revolution brought in by the Federation hit Maranello harder than any other team, especially the obligation to use the same set of tyres for the whole race: that was a notable handicap for the Rosse. The almost monopolistic situation of Bridgestone, which was one of the weapons that favoured Ferrari for years, suddenly transformed itself into a sort of technical isolation – for lack of real and direct terms of comparison – that certainly did not help to resolve the insurgent problems from the first race of the season. There remains the sporadic but significant Indianapolis episode that produced the team's sole victory by Schumacher in a weekend in which Michelin chose the most aggressive approach in relation to the new regulations, which cost the forced forfeit of all the teams that used the French tyres. But apart from that, the cars from Maranello in both the F2004M and F2005 versions were still not up to the opposition, especially Renault and McLaren, which turned out to be the best on the grid. For the first time in many years, the Ferraris were also less reliable, especially with the debut of the F2005, which suffered numerous new concept transmission breakages. One of them was an all-carbon fibre gearbox. The bearings broke because they seized due to their operating temperature during their first few laps. A problem that obliged a careful analysis of the tolerance of the materials used in the gearbox, which had, perhaps, been excessively miniaturised for aerodynamic purposes. The introduction of severe aerodynamic limitations had focused the technicians' efforts to exploit the central channel to create important new developments for the F2005, which, however, negatively influenced the mechanical reliability of the 'box.

The F2005 embodied numerous new features in relation to the previous year's car. They included an all-carbon fibre gearbox instead of one in cast titanium with a carbon fibre skin glued to it (see the 2004 Technical Analy-

V-SHAPED RADIATORS

To reduce bulk, Ferrari also fell into line with Renault and Sauber by mounting their radiators with the double inclination of a V. Note the belt line of the chassis – indicated with an arrow – to remain within the regulations. The other important new Ferrari development can be seen in the detailed illustration of the radiators – exhausts inclined forwards to reduce bulk in the area in front of the wheels.

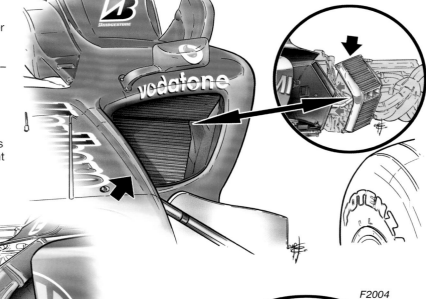

sis), a revolutionary exhaust manifold layout combined with the radiator packs mounted in the V position and inclined forward: these permitted a notable reduction of sections in the central and rear areas of the car, which was also achieved with the help of a sophisticated, made-to-measure braking system produced in collaboration with Brembo. In the field of aerodynamics, it immediately seemed clear just how much Maranello had put its money on a downforce recovery, while its rivals Renault and McLaren were able to build cars that were excellent from the aerodynamics standpoint.

F2004

REAR WING

The newest feature appeared on both the F2004M and the F2005 and was a stepped front wing, described in the aerodynamics chapter. The rear wing also included many new developments right from the official presentation. (1) A mini-plane above the rear axle. (2) Chimneys, the sole purpose of which was to act as guide vanes. (3) Ferrari also used the technique of horizontal cuts in the barge boards, first introduced by Toyota in 2004. (4) There was the possibility of fitting a little wing above the rear light at the car's presentation and the wing was mounted on the car for its first track tests.

ENGINE AND RADIATOR LAYOUT

The new exhaust and engine layout, shown with the system used for earlier Ferraris until the F2004. Note how the exhaust terminals are shorter by about 20 cm, becoming lower and closer to the car body.

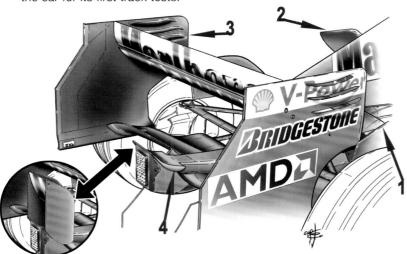

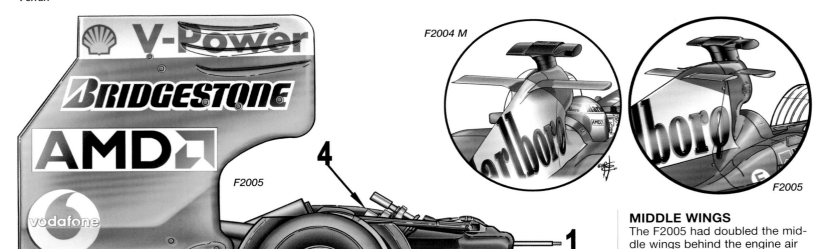

F2004 M

F2005

F2005

MIDDLE WINGS

The F2005 had doubled the middle wings behind the engine air intake in an effort to recover downforce. This was a feature previously reserved solely for especially slow tracks, like Monaco and Budapest.

SAKHIR

At its debut in Bahrain, the F2005 boasted all the features hidden away at its presentation, starting with the appearance of middle wings (2) almost applied to the chimneys (1), which remained the same on the left hand side as those at the car's introduction, but they were open on the right. A middle wing was also mounted at the base of the small plane (3) above the rear light.

CARBON FIBRE GEARBOX

The gearbox of the F2005 was the result of careful miniaturisation in relation to those of the F2004 and the F2004M, which had themselves represented a turnaround for Ferrari in the constructional field. A new technique was introduced with the F2004,

which meant gluing a second skin in carbon fibre around the cast titanium gearbox. On the F2005, the box was made entirely (1) of carbon fibre, with a notable reduction in physical dimensions and without even minimally reducing the unit's

overall rigidity. The cleanliness of the accessories (2) was considerable, especially in the lower area of the gearbox and the suspension layout (4), the latter retaining the Sachs rotating dampers incorporated into the system's rockers. The illustration also shows the new, slightly larger calipers (3), made to Ferrari specifications by Brembo.

SEPANG

For the first time, chimneys were combined with classically shaped shark's gill vents, which came in on the F2002 and were superseded when the inclined chimneys appeared in 2004 at Monaco.

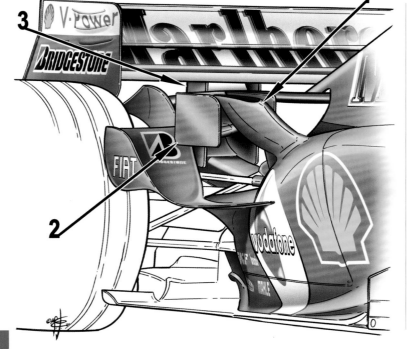

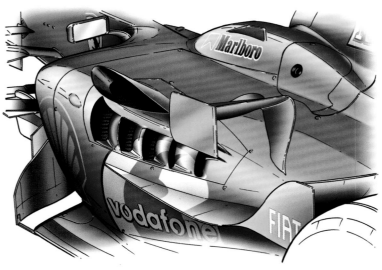

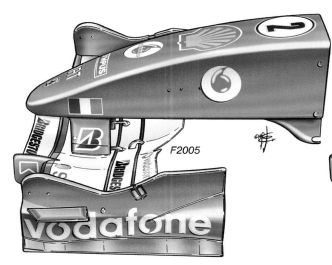

F2005

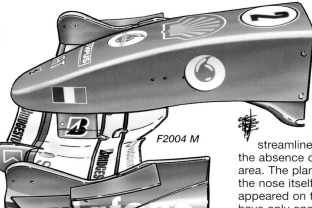

F2004 M

FRONT WING
A comparison of two noses: the one from the presentation of the F2005 – the same as that on the F2004M – and the one tested first at Mugello and then taken to Bahrain. Note how the central area is more streamlined and narrower, but especially the absence of the bulge (1) in the lower area. The planes are, therefore, farther from the nose itself. New developments also appeared on the exterior: the end plates have only one fin instead of two (2) and the one that remained was different, no longer flat but with a multi-faceted surface.

DIFFUSER
The Ferrari's diffuser was new and had a channel (1), which had not previously been seen, added to the upper part of the lateral ones: they came to a halt at the height of the rear axle. This system functioned in combination with the cut in the lateral channels (2), which enabled the car to exploit the central tunnel – only 30 cm wide – of a larger section. Also note the large vertical Gurney flap that had a small ramp at its rear.

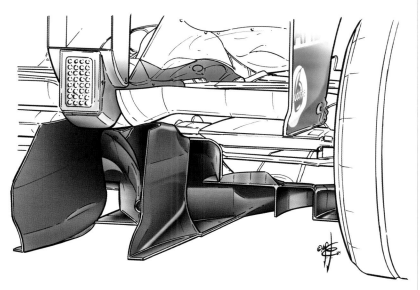

LATERAL BARGE BOARDS
New barge boards behind the front wheels; they were higher but, above all, had this horizontal fin of the Renault school. The dimensions of the chassis were reduced to the limit, due to the use of small devices (1) designed to stay within the minimum measurements imposed with the upper area of the concave chassis.

IMOLA: CHIMNEYS
The F2005 used two different kinds of chimney, both completely closed when seen from the front and with evident aerodynamic functions. On the rear unit, one of the two had a hot air vent in the lower area so as not to interfere with the air flow towards the rear of the car.

REAR WING
The F2005's rear wing was new and different in all its components, even if the most visible modifications concerned the shape of the end plates, which were cut to a greater extent at the height of the flap's trailing edge.

IMOLA
The lower areas of the sidepods were given small forward extensions in a very important area to improve the quality of the air flow towards the rear of the car.

DIFFUSER
The central channel of the diffuser was given an added new diffuser for the purpose of improving the efficiency of the one located at the height of the deformable structure.

BARCELONA: BARGE BOARDS
At Barcelona, a small aerodynamic appendage indicated by the arrow was added to the new barge boards introduced at Imola, just above the one called simply an ashtray.

MONACO
Ferrari placed a load-bearing mini-plane (1) above the suspension's front wishbone, which was slightly cut (2) for Monaco to produce a better steering angle.

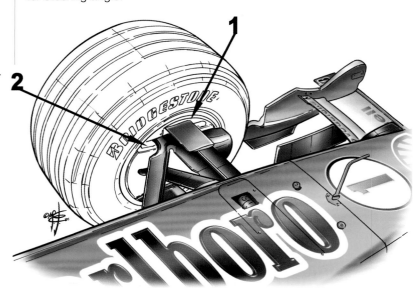

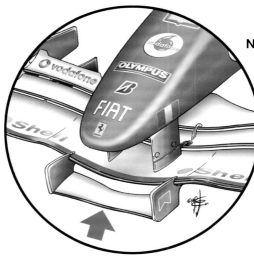

NÜRBURGRING

The Ferraris were given a new front wing, different in all its components. The most apparent modifications included the elimination of the double plane in the central raised area. The principal plane was also different, as was the position of the external fin on the end plate.

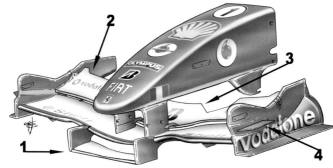

INDY: NOSE

Almost all the teams at Indianapolis retained the developments introduced at Montreal: that was the case with this front wing, which had a new plane that was less stepped at the sides and which had been given an overhanging mini-plane (1) in place of the two seen at Monaco. The flap was the same as the one at Montreal (2), cut in the area near the end plates and with less chord in the spooned centre (3). The end plates were once again given horizontal fins, but of greater length.

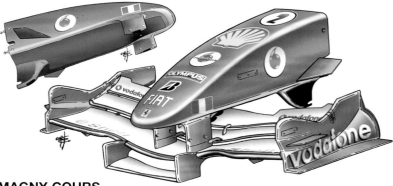

MAGNY COURS

The elimination of red paint from some parts of the car continued in France, where the lower area of the nose and chassis were matt black, as were all the inferior parts of the various aerodynamic appendages. The new nose had additional small triangular fins at the sides and saw the return of the split flap in place of the single element used in Canada and the United States.

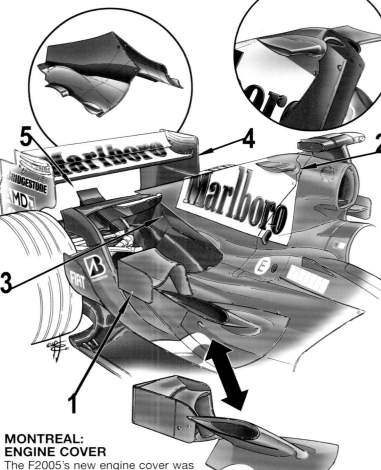

MONTREAL: ENGINE COVER

The F2005's new engine cover was more tapered and, in particular, revised in numerous details. The disposition of the chimneys was new, as were the small lateral winglets, which were now separated and no longer had a blow hole (see below). The four small planes behind the roll bar became two and they brought with them a different cut (2) of the body. The position of the exhausts had also been changed and that required a different barge board set-up (3) in the central area of the body. The rear wing (4) was new and had no link to the mini-planes (5) above the rear light. In the circles are the details of the new "tail" and the different system of mounting the mini-planes behind the roll bar.

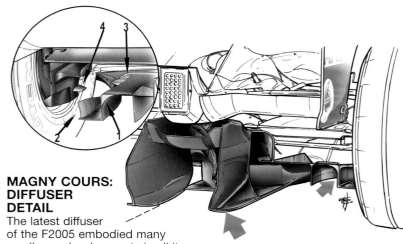

MAGNY COURS: DIFFUSER DETAIL

The latest diffuser of the F2005 embodied many small new developments in all its sectors. Among them were the rounded link (1) with the vertical part of the lateral channel, the barge boards (2) with the rear wheels, which were much higher. At the sides of the lateral channels were small horizontal fins (3) that were also linked. This small horizontal fin (4) was also new and applied to the brake intakes.

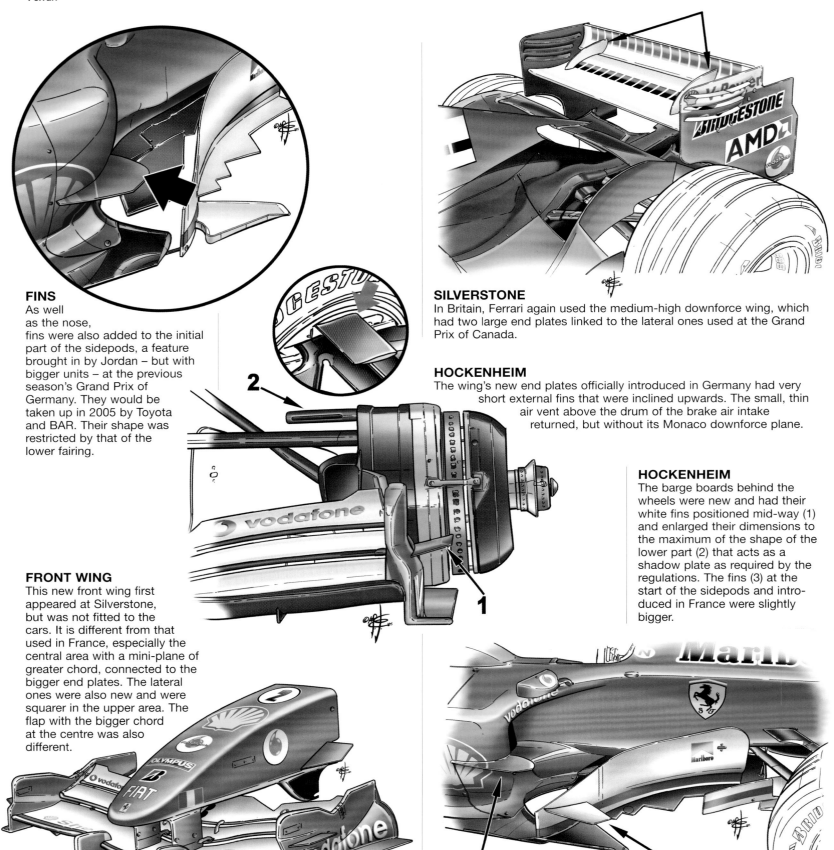

FINS

As well
as the nose,
fins were also added to the initial
part of the sidepods, a feature
brought in by Jordan – but with
bigger units – at the previous
season's Grand Prix of
Germany. They would be
taken up in 2005 by Toyota
and BAR. Their shape was
restricted by that of the
lower fairing.

FRONT WING

This new front wing first
appeared at Silverstone,
but was not fitted to the
cars. It is different from that
used in France, especially the
central area with a mini-plane of
greater chord, connected to the
bigger end plates. The lateral
ones were also new and were
squarer in the upper area. The
flap with the bigger chord
at the centre was also
different.

SILVERSTONE

In Britain, Ferrari again used the medium-high downforce wing, which
had two large end plates linked to the lateral ones used at the Grand
Prix of Canada.

HOCKENHEIM

The wing's new end plates officially introduced in Germany had very
short external fins that were inclined upwards. The small, thin
air vent above the drum of the brake air intake
returned, but without its Monaco downforce plane.

HOCKENHEIM

The barge boards behind the
wheels were new and had their
white fins positioned mid-way (1)
and enlarged their dimensions to
the maximum of the shape of the
lower part (2) that acts as a
shadow plate as required by the
regulations. The fins (3) at the
start of the sidepods and introduced in France were slightly
bigger.

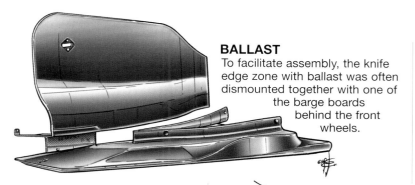

BALLAST
To facilitate assembly, the knife edge zone with ballast was often dismounted together with one of the barge boards behind the front wheels.

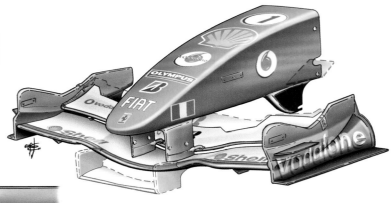

MONZA: FRONT WING
A transparent comparison between the new front wing used at Monza and the one taken to Turkey. Note that the small raised plane in the central 50 cm zone had been eliminated. The flaps have a notably reduced chord. The end plates were also new and straighter, like those of the McLaren.

MONZA: REAR WINGS
A comparison between the three rear wings used by Ferrari at Monza. On the car is the one that competed in the race. The deformable structure (2) of all three was modified and no longer had either the small lateral fin or the mini-wing used for medium and high downforce tracks. All three had new end plates (3) that had a small, forward inclined extension, similar to the one on the F2004. On the right is the wing tested a week earlier, which had a flap with a re-entering trailing edge (1) in the area close to the end plates. On the left is the wing tested only on the Saturday morning by Barrichello, with a notably bigger chord plane and two large middle vanes. Its dimensions and distance from the flap were designed to reduce the effect of the detachment of the air flow near the flap itself.

NEW DIFFUSER
The diffuser plane was further modified in the area near the wheels. The small vertical barge boards, which were previously straight, were now curved upwards, like the connecting part of the lateral channels.

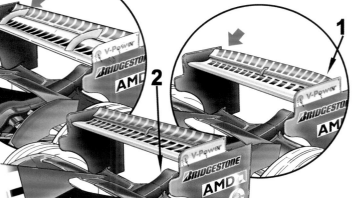

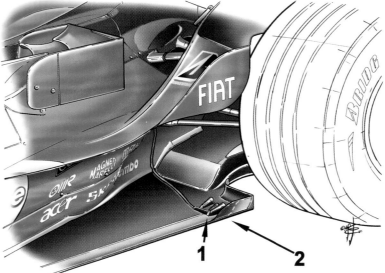

SUZUKA
A small modification in the area in front of the rear wheels with a slightly lengthened external vertical plate (2). Three tyre temperature sensors (1) were used in testing, but only one in the race.

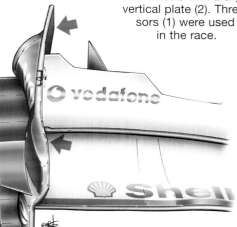

FRONT END PLATES
Ferrari also partially aligned itself with McLaren's less curved, straighter end plates, although they were much inclined towards the interior of the wheels.

:: TOYOTA

CONSTRUCTORS' CHAMPIONSHIP			
	2004	*2005*	
Position	8°	4°	+4 ▲
Points	9	66	+57 ▲

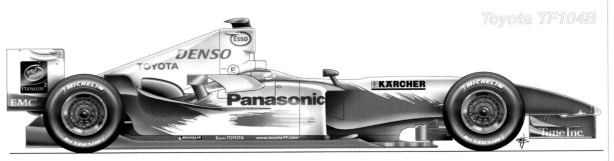

Toyota TF104B

Toyota TF105
presentation

Melbourne

Magny Cours

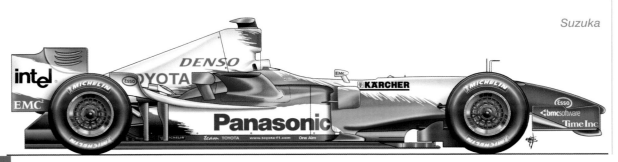

Suzuka

:: For Toyota, 2005 was the coming of age season. The team jumped to fourth place by the end of the championship, with an increase in points compared to 2004 that took it to third place in the hypothetical 'league' table, right behind Renault and McLaren. Much of the credit must go to the new method of work installed by the working party headed by Mike Gascoyne, and their new air tunnel. But credit must also go to the power of the engine designed by Luca Marmorini. Another determinate move in 2005 was the employment of Pascal Vasselon, ex-circuit manager of Michelin.

From the first race of the season, the Toyota TF105B showed itself to be a competitive car, allaying the fears that emerged during its presentation, which said the car had been born old, too much allied to the concepts and shapes expressed in the preceding TF104. The new car at Barcelona appeared to be just a simple and logical development of the concepts embodied in the last TF104B, which was revised and corrected by Mike Gascoyne for the Grand Prix of Germany. Wheelbase, shape of the chassis, titanium gearbox and mechanical installation were practically the same as the 2004 car. The biggest difference concerned the miniaturised rear end due to the new gearbox, more compact exhausts and the lower, more central chimneys.

The rear suspension was also new and had rotating dampers like those of Ferrari, as well as the aerodynamic modifications required by the new regulations. The surprise came during the first race, where the Toyotas sported a new aerodynamic package in an effort to find more downforce. The front wings, turning vanes between the front wheels, sidepods, the two small planes mounted on the forward fins in front of the rear wheels and the rear wing were all new. Development continued during subsequent races, with the introduction in turn of no fewer than five different front wings, including the one taken to Monza. Toyota also introduced a number of new developments illustrated in the aerodynamics chapter. Much work was aimed at obtaining a better weight distribution, with slight variations between the cars of the two drivers: Ralf Schumacher was at ease with a greater division in favour of the front end, while Jarno Trulli was inclined towards the concentration of more weight on the rear axle. A difference that can easily be seen from the outside due to the abundance of ballast in the nose - it even induced the Federation's technicians to keep this expedient under control – and one that was adopted by many teams in an attempt to reduce chronic understeer due to the new aerodynamic limitations imposed by the regulations. The search for greater downforce, possibly without having to give away anything in terms of height from the ground, was one of the most important pursuits during the development of the TF105. As with the previous season, Toyota introduced a B version of their car, even if in this case it was more an experiment carried out for the following season. Seen for the first time during Monza testing, the B derivative that made its racing debut with two examples at the Grand Prix of Japan was mainly a mobile laboratory used to study technical developments for possible incorporation into the 2006 car. The two planes of both the suspension's front wishbones were raised by about 10-12 centimetres so as no longer to have the lower unit anchored to the central bulb, which disturbed the flow of air in the lower area of the car. The whole suspension system was redesigned, its components new. The upright had the central part of its pushrod anchorage separate, so that it could be easily modified in order to find the best solution. All of this with a precise objective: to benefit from the aerodynamic advantages without compromising the mechanical rigidity of the suspension, despite the different

wishbone anchoring system. That development anticipated the definitive elimination of the single keel, scheduled for the TF106 project.

SIDE VIEWS COMPARISON
The new Toyota TF105 that appeared at the official presentation was a logical development of the TF104B, revised and corrected by Mike Gascoyne for the 2004 Grand Prix of Germany, its aerodynamics, obviously, adapted to the new regulations. It had lower sidepods, a new disposition for the chimneys and exhausts. But numerous further new developments had been added to the car by the first race of the 2005 season. They included a heavily spooned front wing, turning vanes between the front wheels, fins in front of the 'pods, chimneys and small flaps high up on the car. The rear wing was also different, but not detectable in relation to the plane. Another evolution of the car was sent to France, with modifications to the fins in front of the sidepods both in the upper and lower parts, the elimination of the small planes behind the roll bar and, in particular, the introduction of vertical fins in the lower rear Coca Cola zone. A B version of the car made its debut in Japan: it had new front suspension similar to that of the McLarens. The fins were also new, doubled and in front of the rear wheels.

Melbourne

Barcelona

SIDEPODS
The TF105's sidepods had the entry aperture further raised from the ground and horizontal fins, which had already been seen during the previous season on the TF104.

MELBOURNE
There was a new aerodynamic package in Australia for Toyota, with the sidepods that incorporated large flaps of the Jordan school, designed by Niccolò Petrucci, who had joined the Cologne team. This first evolution was then followed during the course of the season by another two, which are all compared here.

BARCELONA
A comparison between the further aerodynamic modifications for the TF105 in the sidepod area, with planes applied to the upper area reduced in width (1) to become real spoilers. Below, the horizontal fins have been split (2) and were of a highly sophisticated shape. This area was further modified for Monza, as shown in the appropriate illustration.

ENGINE
Much of the credit for the excellent results achieved by Jarno Trulli and Ralf Schumacher must go to engineer Marmiroli's design of the 10-cylinder engine. Toyota also supplied its power units to a second team in 2005, Jordan.

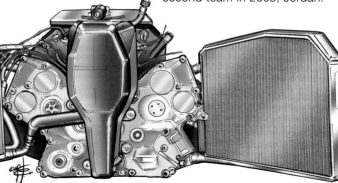

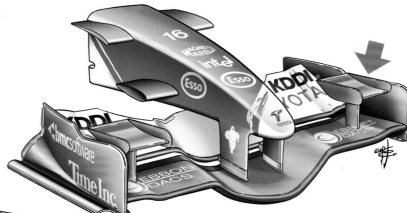

MONACO

The sequence of the different Toyota noses continued with the one used at Monaco, the only unit with two added mini-planes on the front wing, positioned above the principal one and, obviously, part of the search for more downforce for the front end.

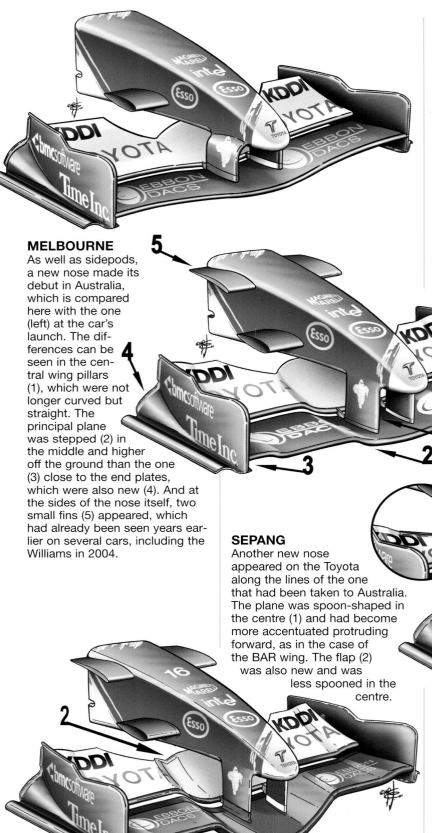

MELBOURNE

As well as sidepods, a new nose made its debut in Australia, which is compared here with the one (left) at the car's launch. The differences can be seen in the central wing pillars (1), which were not longer curved but straight. The principal plane was stepped (2) in the middle and higher off the ground than the one (3) close to the end plates, which were also new (4). And at the sides of the nose itself, two small fins (5) appeared, which had already been seen years earlier on several cars, including the Williams in 2004.

SEPANG

Another new nose appeared on the Toyota along the lines of the one that had been taken to Australia. The plane was spoon-shaped in the centre (1) and had become more accentuated protruding forward, as in the case of the BAR wing. The flap (2) was also new and was less spooned in the centre.

MONZA

The opposite was the case at Monza, where they were looking for a minor advancement resistance. During practice, Toyota experimented with two different types of flap. First the one shown in the circle, then the smaller unit, which was cut at its extremities as shown in the overall illustration. Toyota retained the two small fins at the sides of the central part of the nose in an effort to better direct the air flow towards the rear end of the car.

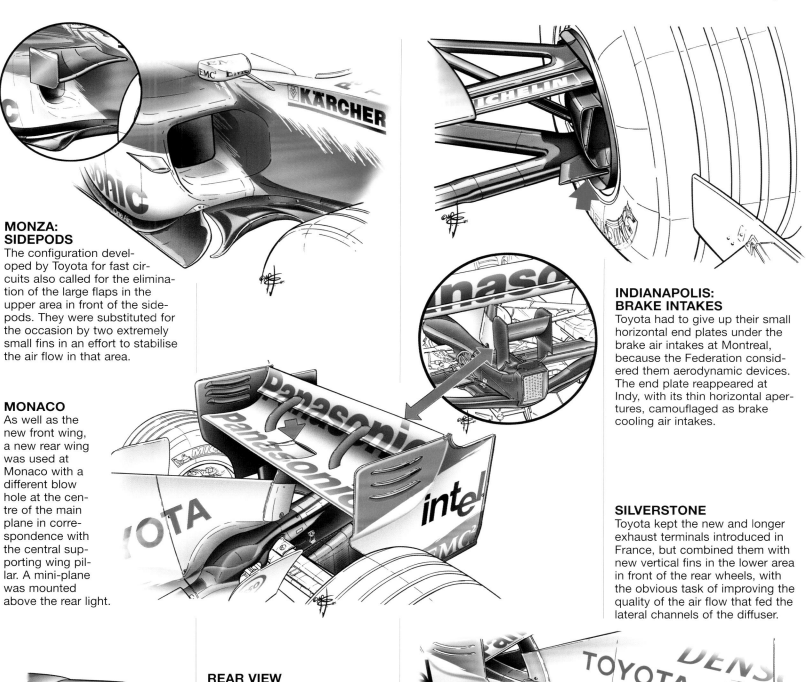

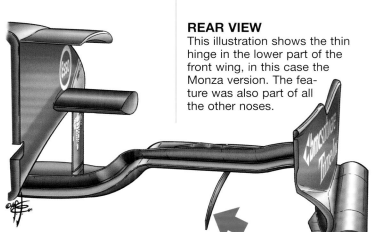

MONZA: SIDEPODS

The configuration developed by Toyota for fast circuits also called for the elimination of the large flaps in the upper area in front of the sidepods. They were substituted for the occasion by two extremely small fins in an effort to stabilise the air flow in that area.

MONACO

As well as the new front wing, a new rear wing was used at Monaco with a different blow hole at the centre of the main plane in correspondence with the central supporting wing pillar. A mini-plane was mounted above the rear light.

INDIANAPOLIS: BRAKE INTAKES

Toyota had to give up their small horizontal end plates under the brake air intakes at Montreal, because the Federation considered them aerodynamic devices. The end plate reappeared at Indy, with its thin horizontal apertures, camouflaged as brake cooling air intakes.

SILVERSTONE

Toyota kept the new and longer exhaust terminals introduced in France, but combined them with new vertical fins in the lower area in front of the rear wheels, with the obvious task of improving the quality of the air flow that fed the lateral channels of the diffuser.

REAR VIEW

This illustration shows the thin hinge in the lower part of the front wing, in this case the Monza version. The feature was also part of all the other noses.

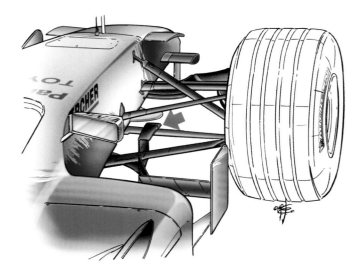

ISTANBUL: DIFFUSER

The new diffuser plane with a modified cut of the central channel (3). The lateral channels were practically unchanged, but had two middle vanes (2), even though the illustration only shows one; the same goes for the rounded screening (1) in the zone near the tyre.

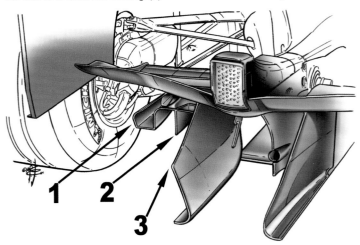

ISTANBUL

As Toyota waited for the B version of the TF105 with the higher anchorage of the front suspension wishbones, they took to Turkey a number of slight modifications to the combination of the small turning vanes, linked to the flaps in the upper area of the entrance to the side-pods.

SUZUKA: FRONT VIEW COMPARISON WITH THE TF105B

An earlier debut for the B version of the car had a higher front suspension so as to eliminate the central keel from the chassis of the future TF106, which, at that moment, remained (1) as a compromise solution so as not to have to build a completely new chassis. Both the wishbones had been raised (1-2) as can be seen in the comparison with the new TF105B on the right. The steering column (3-4) had also been raised as it had created problems for the drivers, especially Trulli. The turning vanes (5-6) were also different and no longer interrupted by the presence of the lower wishbone.

SUZUKA

All three of the Toyotas at Suzuka, including the spare car, still had the old chassis, but with modified aerodynamics in the zone ahead of the rear wheels, double vertical fins (in the circle) to keep the air flow directed to the area inside the wheels and, as much as possible, towards the rear of the car.

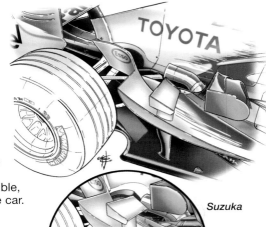

Suzuka

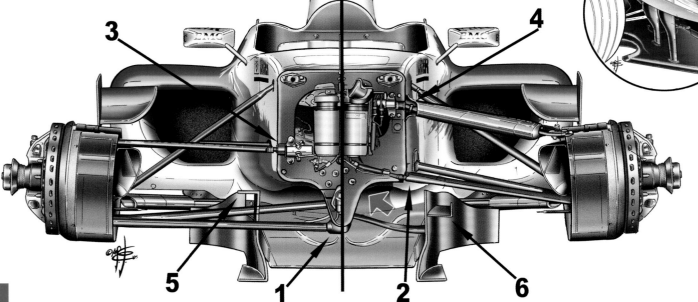

WILLIAMS

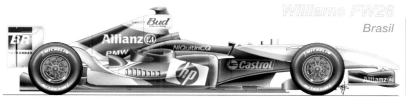
Williams FW26
Brasil

Williams FW27
presentation

Magny Cours

San Paolo

team; the facility eventually came into operation in April 2004, but it was only calibrated to perfection in August 2005. And all of this at the time of the weighty revolution in aerodynamics introduced by the Federation, which meant an incredible amount of work had to be carry out in – the wind tunnel. With the FW27, Williams had also thrown out the work carried out the previous year by Antonia Terzi, who was replaced by Loic Bigois. The single keel was back and connected to a front part that was fairly classic. The high nose was of characteristic design, with the lower area heavily concave to permit a notable incidence of the flaps, linked to a spooned plane of extreme shape. The only connection the FW27 had with its predecessor was its turning vanes inside the front axle, of which it retained most of the elements. The most significant new aspect of the car were the dimensions of the sidepods: they were at least 8-10 cm lower than those of the FW25, but more than anything else much different to the ones seen on the majority of their adversaries' cars, which had opted for high and rounded entry mouths. The abandonment of the twin keel also permitted a significant saving in terms of weight, so that an overall slimming course aimed at all sectors of the car enabled the FW27 to take on about 60 kg of ballast. A new body (Mk2) came in at the Grand Prix of France and meant the reconstruction of the chassis, both of which were

A second seriously negative season cost Williams its premature divorce from BMW, the official supplier of its engines. But even so, Didcot worked in an incredible manner throughout the season, introducing a withering series of over 130 modifications during the year, including two body versions and ten different front wings. There were the same number of new features for the rear of the car, with the appearance of four or five diffusers as well as a myriad of fins and small winglets spread more or less all over the car. The modifications, brought from the factory by hand at the last minute, were often mounted on the car by the Williams technicians on the Saturday. In theory, the poor results obtained by the British team do not justify a long review on the FW27, which was even more unique than the FW26 with its walrus nose, a car born badly. But the efforts of the team, which was now back under the direction of Patrick Head again with Sam Michael in charge at the race tracks, deserve an ample account even if, obviously, incomplete due to the multiplicity of developments taken to the circuits. The problems experienced in establishing the new wind tunnel worked against the English

SINGLE KEEL

The chassis of the FW27 no longer had twin keels, which were the origin of the walrus nose. The lower triangle was anchored (1) again to a central bulb. The knife-edge area (2) that was first flat was convex – as on the 2004 BAR – and hid much ballast so as to concentrate greater weight on the front axle. The turning vanes (3) were of the FW26 type, which had an external mini-channel at the level of the reference plane.

85

raced at the following Grand Prix of Great Britain: Webber competed with the Mk2 version and Heidfeld with the old body. From the next Grand Prix of Germany, the team concentrated on new developments that included vents in the upper part of the engine cover similar to those of the Renaults in both the fields of cooling and aerodynamic efficiency. Many experiments were begun with the front wing, at the end of which the Williams unit became almost a photocopy of those of McLaren, with upper deck flaps. The experiment carried out on integrating the rear brake air intakes with the new diffuser planes was also interesting.

LOW SIDEPODS

The most surprising aspect of the new FW27 was the drastic reduction in the height of its sidepods, the shape of which was inspired by the version that came out in Belgium in 2004 (see that year's Technical Analysis). The fins in front of the rear wheels (1) were much shorter and the engine cover terminated considerably lower and the exhaust chimneys (2), which were smaller. The planes behind the roll bar (3) had become four instead of the FW26's two, but the chimneys (4) were even larger and severely inclined outwards so as not to interfere with the air flow towards the rear wing. The engine air intake was incredibly small (5) and caught its air in an area farther away, undisturbed by the turbulence from the helmet.

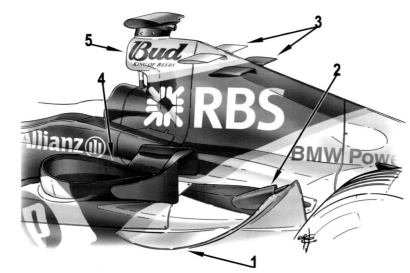

MINI-PLANES

In their search for more down-force, Williams placed two mini-planes 15 cm wide above the rear light. A feature that had been used by Arrows at Monaco in the past, but the planes were in front of the rear wing group.

MELBOURNE

A new front wing for the Williams, which had this triangular fin that we had already seen on the 2001 Sauber and Williams.

END PLATES

Further development of the front wing end plates with a new, differently shaped fin, compared to the one seen in Australia: it was slightly bigger, less inclined but had a section of greater wing profile and was concave. The external fin was a little different, too; the flap was also new and, comprised a mixed solution incorporating aspects of the one previously seen in Australia.

Melbourne

Sepang

SEPANG

To improve heat dissipation, Renault style vents (2) were added to the sidepods and there was a small fin (1) under the bigger chimneys.

SAKHIR

Among the many new Williams developments were the barge boards in front of the sidepods, introduced in Malaysia and raised to about 4 cm, while remaining exactly the same shape.

ENGINE COVER

The racing version of the FW27's engine cover was considerably modified. The terminal area was cut (1) and the wide plane above the gearbox, which was anchored to the old engine cover, was dropped. There was a central vent (2) in the new cover to improve the evacuation of the hot air. The car also had symmetrical but very high chimneys (3); the rear wing was also new and had stepped end plates (4) similar to those of Toyota.

END PLATES

Developments of the front wing end plates were came into play at every race, with various internal and external fin typologies; this with a view to finding the most effective union with the front wheels, which were closer due to the raising of the planes, now nearer the centre of the tyres.

BARCELONA

On the Friday, Williams used a new front wing and barge boards modified at the point indicated, with the addition of a further "tooth", which protruded from the flat section down low.

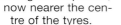

Sepang

Barhain

BARCELONA

On the Saturday, new engine covers arrived that had only been determined in the wind tunnel on the Wednesday after the Grand Prix of Imola and produced in just seven days. There were just two and they had two flaps in the area ahead of the rear wheels (previously smooth), with a small vertical fin (2) seen in Australia in a more curled form, and a doubling of planes in the zone behind the chimneys (3), as on the new Minardi.

MONACO

There was a new front wing for the FW27, with its principal plane slightly raised at the edges in the anchorage point with an end plate, as shown in the yellow portion.

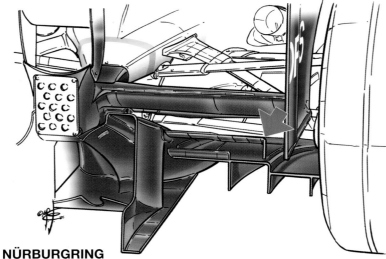

NÜRBURGRING
From the Grand Prix of Monaco, Williams brought in a small wing plane above the lateral channels of the diffuser, a feature that Red Bull adopted from the start of the year and that was introduced into F1 by Egbhal Hamidy at the time of Stewart in 1999.

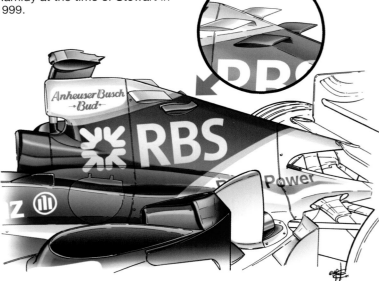

END PLATES
The umpteenth version of end plates for the rear wing, with an external fin (1) that no longer had a wing plane. The low knife edge of the plane was not straight but completely round this time.

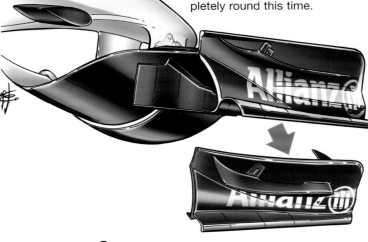

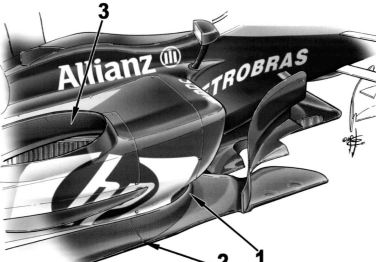

WINGLETS
The four new small winglets, which first appeared at Monaco, were retained as they delivered greater downforce effect. The second, especially, had a more "loaded" plane, as can be seen in the comparison with the old solution shown in the circle.

MAGNY COURS
New aerodynamics appeared in France, with much more concave sidepods in the lower area (1) and the air intake raised in relation to the previous version. The underbody was for the first time divided into two parts, with the front knife-edge zone separate. The chimneys were new, lower and more inclined towards the exterior. The illustration also shows the new radiators.

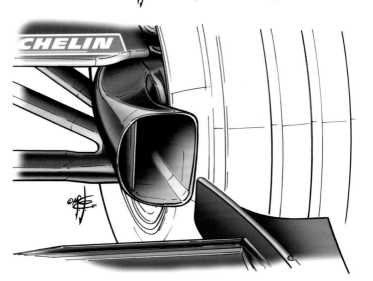

MONTREAL
A new air intake with a bigger section was adopted for the circuits hardest on the brakes.

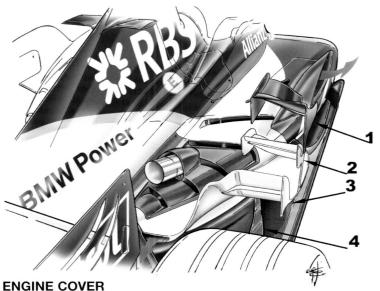

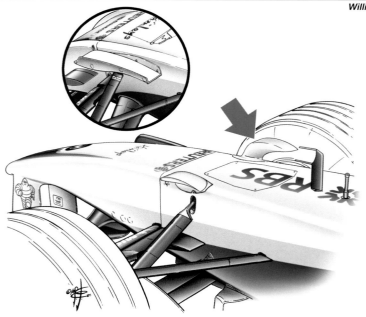

ENGINE COVER

The means of dissipating hot air from the sidepods was completely different. Gone were the large chimneys to make way for a series of thin vents similar to those of Renault. Note the slender terminal vent indicated by the arrow. The body was very narrow in the lower area (1) and had an added upper deck flap (2) positioned before the one in front of the rear wheels (3). But this vertical fin (4) in the lower area was retained.

SILVERSTONE

Williams introduced these ears – very similar to those used by Renault – on their Mk2 car from the Spanish until the Canadian Grand Prix. The illustration shows fins similar to those fitted the previous year from the Grand Prix of France, the task of which was to move the centre of aerodynamic pressure towards the centre rear zone of the car. Those ears were positioned higher on the FW27 in function with the raised position of the front wing group.

SILVERSTONE: OLD SIDEPODS

Williams decided to carry out an experiment at Silverstone during qualifying on the Saturday and the race on Sunday by dismantling Heidfeld's usual car with new aerodynamics and assembling a spare, old type chassis with aerodynamics first used prior to the Grand Prix of France. The internal fluid dynamics were different, with the old vertical air vent (1) in the terminal zone of the sidepods. The exhausts (2) were given chimneys – the one on the left was bigger – with a smaller flap (3) between the two sidepod elements.

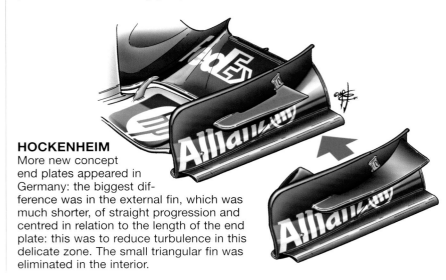

HOCKENHEIM

More new concept end plates appeared in Germany: the biggest difference was in the external fin, which was much shorter, of straight progression and centred in relation to the length of the end plate: this was to reduce turbulence in this delicate zone. The small triangular fin was eliminated in the interior.

NEW BARGE BOARDS

New barge boards for the B version of the FW27. They were lower (1), as can be seen on the left in a comparison shown in yellow with the old solution. The lower part was practically unchanged and had an ample stepped area (2) with a small mini-skirt that descended to the level of the reference plane.

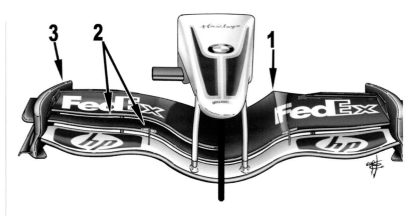

BUDAPEST

Williams and Toyota came out simultaneously
with a series of six planes behind the roll bar in place of the usual four, in their search for a few more kilograms of downforce. As can be seen in the illustrations, the two versions are different on the Williams; only the initial taller ones fully exploited the maximum width of 50 cm permitted by the regulations; the other two were smaller, descending in steps and had negative lift mini-planes armed with small Gurney flaps, shown in yellow. All six of those on Toyota were of maximum width and also had a downwards-stepped progression.

UPPER DECK FLAP

Another surprise from Williams was the umpteenth aerodynamic solution sent into action without ever having been tried on the track. This one was the upper deck flap (2), as used by McLaren and Ferrari at the start of the year: its task was to avoid the detachment of the fluid vein beyond a certain angle of incidence in relation to the version with a single flap (1) shown on the right. The end plates were also new and followed the road taken by McLaren in a less extreme way of the inner alignment with the front wheels. It was noted that the 2005 tyres tended to lose little particles of rubber that deposited themselves on the end plates, diminishing their effectiveness.

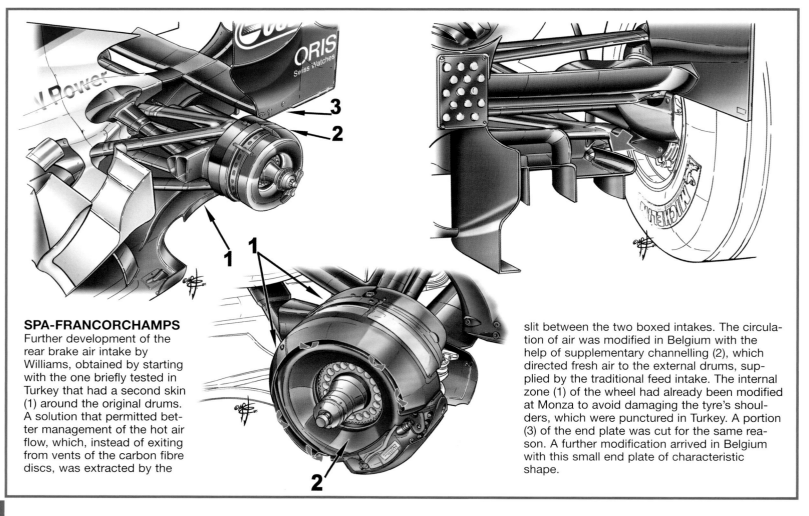

SPA-FRANCORCHAMPS

Further development of the rear brake air intake by Williams, obtained by starting with the one briefly tested in Turkey that had a second skin (1) around the original drums. A solution that permitted better management of the hot air flow, which, instead of exiting from vents of the carbon fibre discs, was extracted by the slit between the two boxed intakes. The circulation of air was modified in Belgium with the help of supplementary channelling (2), which directed fresh air to the external drums, supplied by the traditional feed intake. The internal zone (1) of the wheel had already been modified at Monza to avoid damaging the tyre's shoulders, which were punctured in Turkey. A portion (3) of the end plate was cut for the same reason. A further modification arrived in Belgium with this small end plate of characteristic shape.

ISTANBUL

Williams had been studying the McLaren's front wing for some time. The first result was seen in Hungary with the upper deck flap; the straight end plates (2) arrived in Turkey, no longer curved and with a simpler principal plane (1) similar to the spoon shaped one of the MP4-20. The new external fins were also longer and thinner (3). This was Williams' 10th version of its front wing to be introduced during the 2005 season.

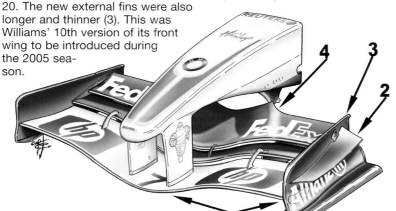

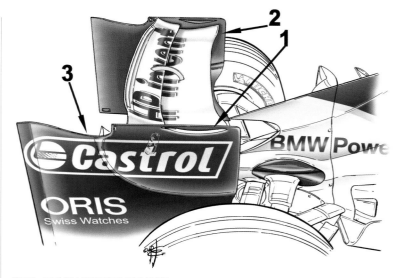

SPA-FRANCORCHAMPS

As at Monza, the fast circuit wing was used at Spa with a sole slit of the Toyota school (1), a principal plane (2) slightly raised at the edges and the barge boards cut in the terminal area to reduce vortices in that zone (3).

SUZUKA

The umpteenth new nose for Williams: the Japanese version was inspired by that of Renault due to the presence of a raised flap, connected in this case to the internal part of the end plate (on the R25 it was an integral part of the end plate itself). As in the case of the Renault, its purpose was not to increase load on the front end but to direct the air flow so that it went higher to positively influence the efficiency of the rear wing.

WING COMPARISON

A comparison between the wing introduced in Hungary (above) and the one in Turkey. Both have upper deck flaps, but the main characteristic of the new solution was the abandonment of the curved receding progression of the barge boards. Now, they were both straight (1), like those of the McLaren MP4-20 and had long, thin external fins (2). The main plane was simpler (3) and higher in the central zone, where the old unit had a double curvature (4) that was heavily spoon shaped.

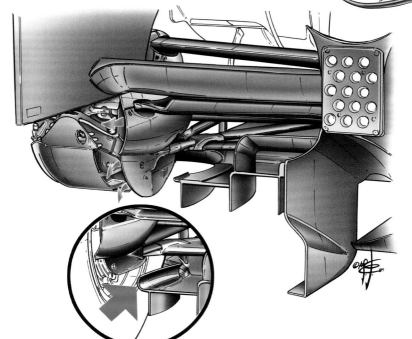

SHANGHAI

Further modification to the external channel of the diffuser in relation to the version seen in Brazil (shown in the circle), introduced together with the modification to the brake and disc air intake, which first appeared in Turkey and turned up again in Japan. Now, there were internal vents, as indicated by the arrows.

BAR

CONSTRUCTORS' CLASSIFICATION			
	2004	2005	
Position	2°	7°	-5 ▼
Points	119	34	-85 ▼

BAR 006
Brasil

BAR 007
presentation

Montreal

Suzuka

The 2005 season was one to forget for BAR Honda after its excellent performance the previous year, when the Anglo-Japanese team came second in the constructors' championship. It was an effort that cost the team a great deal and obliged it to sacrifice the creation of the new car in favour of developing the 006 until the last race. To that was added a problem discovered in setting up the wind tunnel that made the team lose precious time in the elaboration of models of the car. On its track debut, the 007 immediately manifested difficulty in aerodynamic balance, so

much so that during the early races there were front wings and barge boards behind the wheels, inspired by those of the previous season. On top of all this, there were certain complications in adapting to the new Michelin tyres, especially during races, but the severe after effects of overall yield also had the noted regulation problems after Imola, which banished the squad from the circuits and disorientated its top technicians. The team was prohibited from competing in two Grands Prix, a matter which is analysed in the Controversies chapter of this book. Not even the Honda 10-cylinder engine was immune from the defects in a season in which power units were required to withstand two consecutive races. A real shame, because right from its unveiling the new 007 showed a notable sophistication in its aerodynamics, which could be seen in every single detail starting with the lower wishbones of the front suspension that had become real variable section wing planes. Then there were the refined turning vanes, which brought together all the new steps seen in 2004: double vanes between the front wheels like McLaren, horizontal fins like the old BAR and others of the Renault school connecting the sidepods. In this sector, the BAR Honda was updated at almost every Grand Prix. Each of the sidepods turned out to be extremely narrow at 8-10 cm less, and they included a sort if horizontal stepped area to better channel the air flow in the rear, where narrowing in the so-called Coke bottle zone was even more pronounced. This was a result obtained due to the different installation of the radiators, which had a double inclination and took on the external shape of the sidepods.

The 007 had a slightly shorter wheelbase as a result of the greater compactness of the engine-gearbox group, despite a fuel tank that could have had a slightly bigger capacity. The gearbox was second generation compared to the carbon fibre component introduced in 2004: lighter and more compact, the 2005 'box ensured less complex production – eight were planned at the start of the season – but more than anything else it took advantage of speeds and a management system produced by Honda itself. The quick shift mechanism meant gear changes could be made in almost zero time.

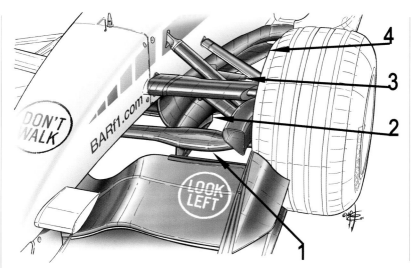

GUIDE VANES

The 007 began the season with a guide vane layout in the front wheel area that was inspired simultaneously by the units used on previous BARs as well as on the McLarens and Renaults. The triangular fin (1) was already on the 2004 BAR, while the double barge boards (2-3) were of the McLaren school. The horizontal fin (3) connected to them was new, while the one anchored to

FRONT SUSPENSION

Refinement in the team's aerodynamic research could be seen in all the details of the BAR 007. The carbon fibre front suspension had winged sections (1) with a different chord. The guide vanes (2) used at the start of the season were double and of the McLaren school, while the triangular fin (3) that was on the 2004 BAR remained. The series of horizontal fins in front of the sidepods (4) were new, their purpose to direct a greater quantity of air flow towards the central channel of the diffuser.

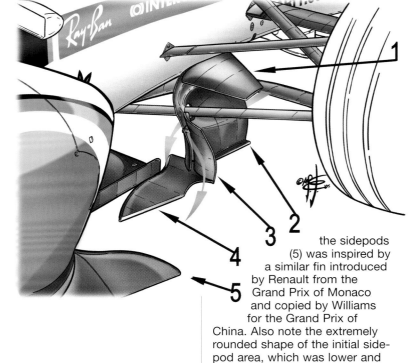

the sidepods (5) was inspired by a similar fin introduced by Renault from the Grand Prix of Monaco and copied by Williams for the Grand Prix of China. Also note the extremely rounded shape of the initial sidepod area, which was lower and squared on the BAR.

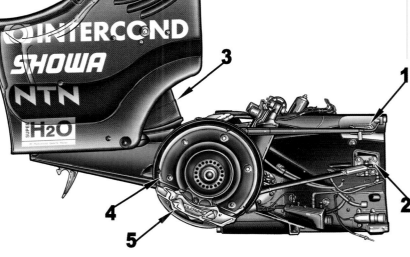

2004

CARBON FIBRE GEARBOX

The BAR 007 retained its carbon fibre gearbox with slight modifications to simplify its production. The suspension mounts (1) were made more rigid and also had different anti-squat values (2). The rear wing group was supported by a central pylon (3). The illustration shows the version used during the last Grands Prix of the season, when BAR fitted Japanese Akebono brake calipers (5) instead of the British Alcons. The team did not use external drums but simple flat covers (4), which were not on the 2004 car.

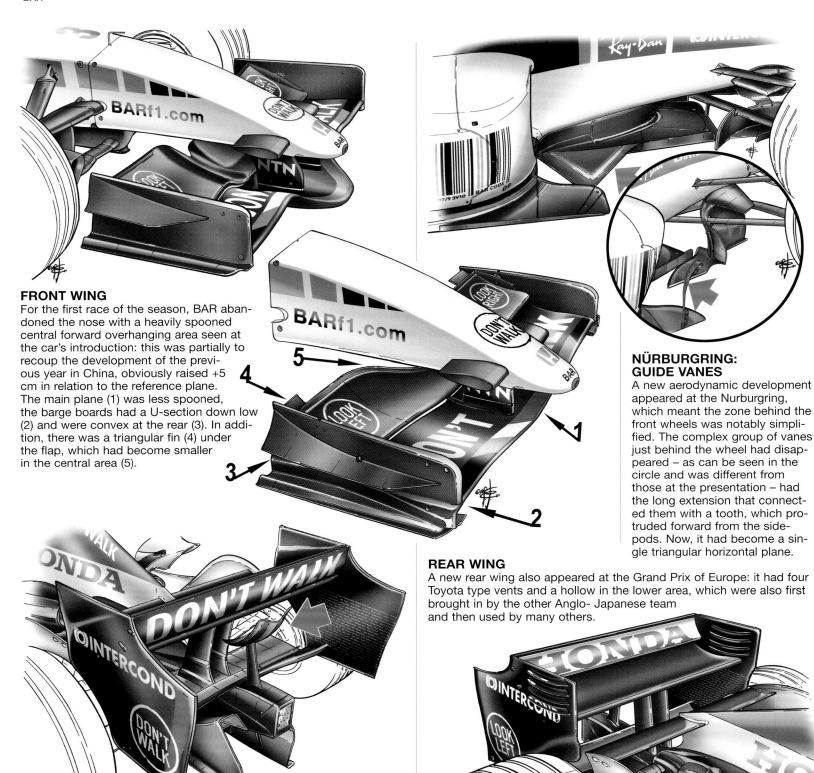

FRONT WING

For the first race of the season, BAR abandoned the nose with a heavily spooned central forward overhanging area seen at the car's introduction: this was partially to recoup the development of the previous year in China, obviously raised +5 cm in relation to the reference plane. The main plane (1) was less spooned, the barge boards had a U-section down low (2) and were convex at the rear (3). In addition, there was a triangular fin (4) under the flap, which had become smaller in the central area (5).

NÜRBURGRING: GUIDE VANES

A new aerodynamic development appeared at the Nurburgring, which meant the zone behind the front wheels was notably simplified. The complex group of vanes just behind the wheel had disappeared – as can be seen in the circle and was different from those at the presentation – had the long extension that connected them with a tooth, which protruded forward from the sidepods. Now, it had become a single triangular horizontal plane.

REAR WING

A new rear wing also appeared at the Grand Prix of Europe: it had four Toyota type vents and a hollow in the lower area, which were also first brought in by the other Anglo- Japanese team and then used by many others.

IMOLA

The team had a new aerodynamic package for Imola, beginning with this curious triangular appendage positioned above the rear light. The diffuser plane was also new and had a lower central channel that was sloped in the terminal area.

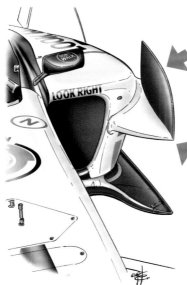

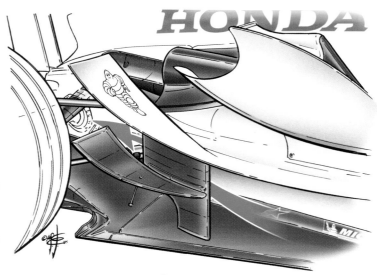

MONTREAL: SIDEPODS

New winglets of the Jordan and Toyota persuasion appeared on the upper part of the BAR sidepods. Their shape was determined on the basis of the lower horizontal fin, because the regulations said that any protrusion that jutted out from the chassis had to have its own shadow plate at 5 cm from the reference plane. The end plates were especially large and were also vaguely triangular.

MONTREAL: REAR FINS

BAR brought back a feature that had already been tested the previous year in the Grand Prix of France. It comprised large fins located in front of the rear wheels with an added triangular plane of downforce effect and was the same as those on the Williams and Renault.

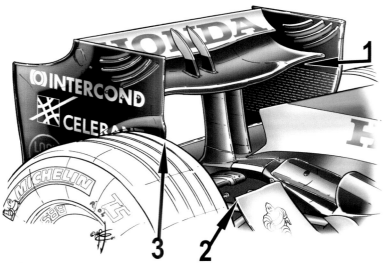

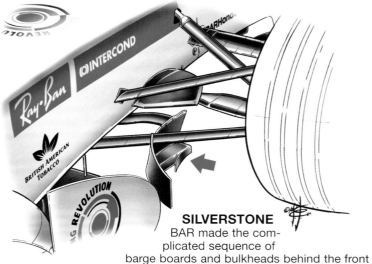

INDY: REAR WING

The team kept the same medium-to-low load wing brought in at Montreal: it was vaguely spoon shaped with its central zone (1) lower so as to create more efficiency in that area in relation to the one close to the end plates, which had cuts in the upper area of the front, first used by Toyota and copied by many other teams. It should be mentioned that there are no longer any lateral extensions inside the wheels (2). The end plates of the wing formed a small recessed stepped area (3).

SILVERSTONE

BAR made the complicated sequence of barge boards and bulkheads behind the front wheels more linear. They fitted a double element linked to the new triangular fins introduced at the Grand Prix of Canada; inside, they were painted with the national flags of their two drivers. A further refinement to improve the quality of the air flow towards the rear of the car.

ISTANBUL

While waiting to bring in important new aerodynamic developments, which would be used during the subsequent three Grands Prix, BAR employed various typologies of vents to dissipate the extreme heat generated by the Turkish track. The illustration shows the two most extreme versions plus a third, more closed solution, which, in the perspective of the picture, hides its opening under the lateral flaps.

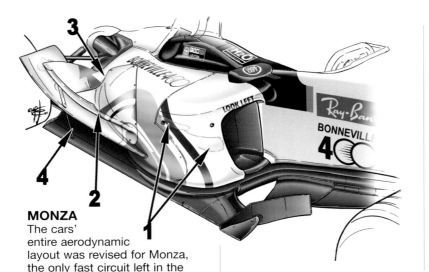

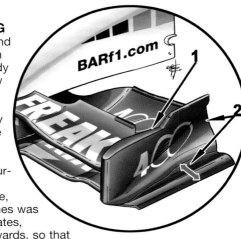

SAO PAOLO: FRONT WING

In Brazil, BAR fielded the second version of its front wing with an upper deck flap that had already been seen in Belgium. The new aspect of it concerned, in particular, the concave end plates at mid-length (1), but especially more inclined inwards (2) in the rear so as to have a different alignment with the tyres and reduce the harmful effects of turbulence created by the covers. Following the McLaren example, the total width of the wing planes was reduced to position the end plates, which were heavily inclined inwards, so that they optimised the air flow towards the car's body.

MONZA

The cars' entire aerodynamic layout was revised for Monza, the only fast circuit left in the world championship. As well as new front and rear wings, the sidepods were also modified. The Jordan-style fins (1), the vertical units in front of the rear wheels characteristic of BAR (2) and the semi-horizontal (4) in the low area were all eliminated. The hot air vents were partially closed.

SPA-FRANCORCHAMPS: FRONT WING

BAR went to Belgium with a nose that had an upper deck flap and which was very similar to those of Sauber during the season, but they were only used during winter private testing before the start of the championship. This feature was taken to a track where Renault chose to use the same Monza wing, but without the double flap that came in at Imola and was retained for the Grand Prix of Italy.

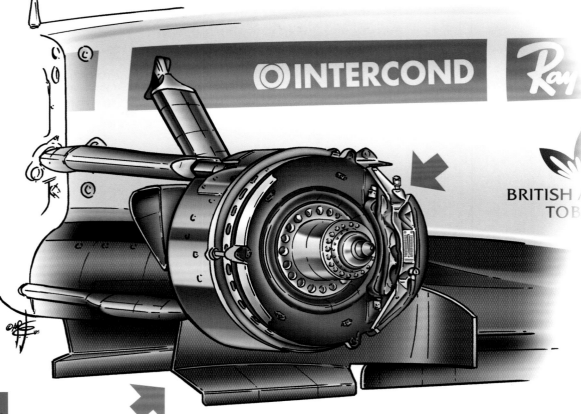

SUZUKA

For Suzuka, BAR set a completely new trend. It debuted its new brake caliper supplier Akebono of Japan, whose products were used instead of the usual Alcons the team had fitted exclusively since 2004. The calipers were easily recognisable by the golden colour of their internal area. Note that the inclination of the guide vanes remained the same. The suspension was also new and comprised various uprights made by Honda in Metalmatrix.

⠿RED BULL

Red Bull's debut car was, obviously, based on the previous season's Jaguar and favourably impressed, in part because the start of the 2005 season revealed itself to be rather difficult for Ferrari, BAR and Williams. Designed and built under the direction of two technicians who joined the team from Renault, Mark Smith and the aerodynamic specialist Ben Agathangelous, the RB1 was certainly not among the most beautiful cars of the season . Its voluminous shape, with high, square sidepods, were in against the current trend in relation to the new cars, which were more streamlined especially in the lower area of the 'pods. The new RB1, however, did show itself to be competitive, especially in qualifying; but the situation often changed during the race, even if 38 points at the end of the season is no mean feat for a team making its debut. The excessive wear rate of the rear tyres was one of the cars' main problems and attempts were made to obviate this performance shortcoming, in part with continuous modifications to the division of weight and the anti-skid system. There were two important phases in the development of the car during the season: the one seen at the Grand Prix of France, where new rear aerodynamics were introduced, and the Grand Prix of Hungary where a new engine cover the terminal part of which was pointed and cut made its debut. Red Bull especially attracted attention for the prominent aerodynamic fairing on the suspension arms, created by exploiting to the limit the regulation concerned, to the point that the units seemed real wing planes.

SAKHIR

There were bigger air vents for the Red Bull's enormous chimneys, which were longer and farther forward, in line with the very traditional position of the radiator packs. Note how the exhaust chimneys were also rather high.

Jaguar R5

Red Bull RB1
presentation

San Paolo

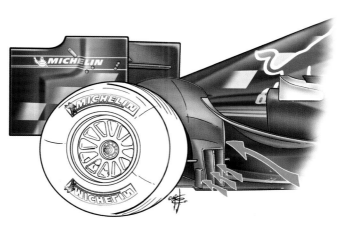

FINS

Links with the old Jaguar were significant and can also be seen in a comparison of planes. There was no surprise in the conservation one of the new features brought in by the old British team in 2004: the vertical fins in the zone that narrowed in front of the rear wheels. In the version raced at the start of the year, the car had two vertical vents, which were later dropped mid-way through the season.

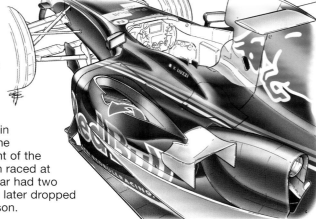

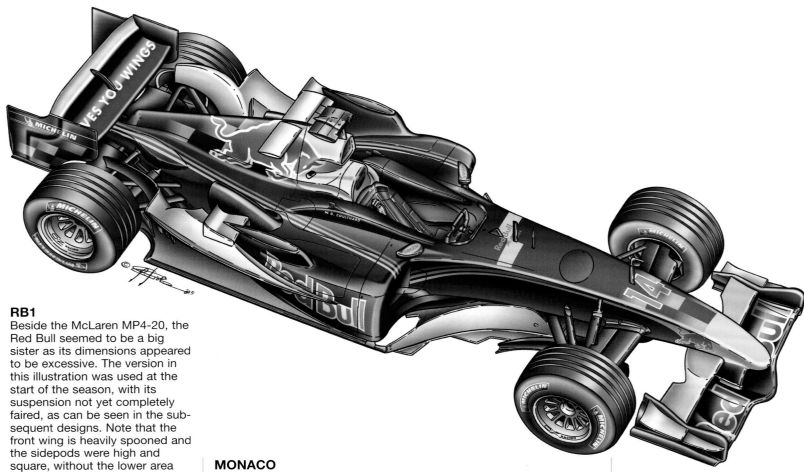

RB1

Beside the McLaren MP4-20, the Red Bull seemed to be a big sister as its dimensions appeared to be excessive. The version in this illustration was used at the start of the season, with its suspension not yet completely faired, as can be seen in the subsequent designs. Note that the front wing is heavily spooned and the sidepods were high and square, without the lower area being concave as required by the new trend exhibited by the 2005 car.

MONACO

The front end of the Red Bull was also given a single, large wing plane, which included a front arm of the upper wishbone and a steering link in order to form a true wing plane. This development made its impact, so much so that it was discussed at a meeting of the WTG after the Grand Prix of Canada, where it was pronounced legal. At the same meeting, the brake air intake was also discussed, as it had become an increasingly mobile aerodynamic appendage (see the Controversies chapter).

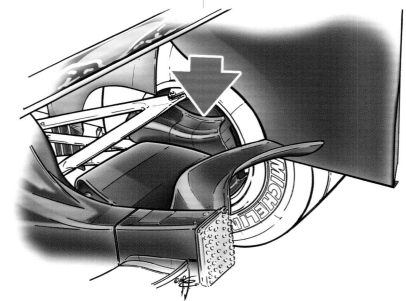

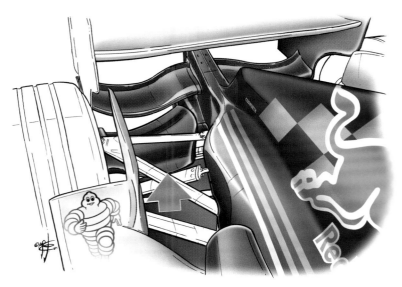

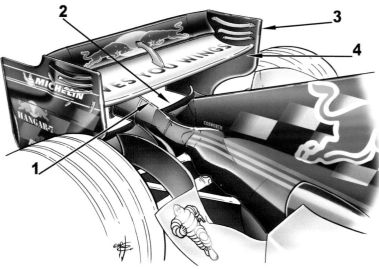

MONACO

The considerable suspension fairing of the rear suspension made its debut at Monaco and was even bigger than at the first race, when it was judged to be the most comprehensive of all the competing cars. In practice, this plane, with its very large section applied around the drive shaft and the toe-in link, worked in harmony with the diffuser.

BUDAPEST

Red Bull took a new engine cover to Hungary, which terminated in a point, like the one introduced in Germany by Renault and was also narrower in the areas at the side of the gearbox. The entire rear wing group was also new and had end plates with a considerable number of vents of the Toyota style applied to all the cars, even if with some differences.

MAGNY COURS

New rear aerodynamics made their debut at the Grand Prix of France, starting with the wing supporting deformable structure (1) of triangular section. The lower plane (2) was also new; the end plates of the wing were given Toyota-type cuts (3), while both the principal plane and flap had no completely straight progression but a curved one (4) in the area near the end plates.

MONZA

At the only fast circuit in the world championship, Red Bull was the team that fielded the least traditional rear wing. The especially unloaded plane was arrow shaped at the leading edge so as to have a more negative lift surface in the more efficient central area. In this zone, the plane raises itself up slightly. Note the three large end plates much detached from the flap and with the task of providing more rigidity to the whole, without penalising air flow.

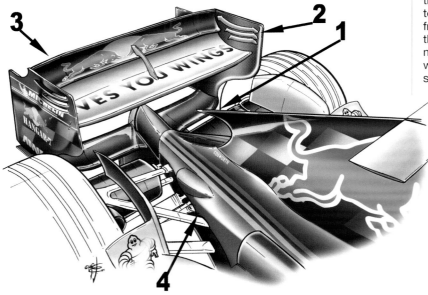

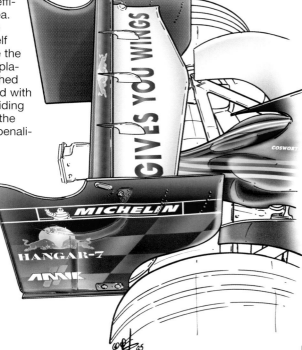

SAUBER

Sauber C23

Sauber C24
presentation

Melbourne

Silverstone

included a new underbody, a rear wing of different conception and especially the new engine cover, which produced good results. Barcelona was the stage on which the vane under the chassis, the front turning vanes and return, as well as new brake air intakes. The rear end of the car was also renewed for Istanbul. The last two developments arrived for Monza, with the classic aerodynamic configuration for fast circuits and at Spa there were new front and rear wings. With BMW's acquisition of the team, the Ferrari engine supply situation obviously came to an end, which also involved the gearbox in 2004 with evident influence on the general philosophy of the car, which was based on the previous F2003-GA. On the other hand, the C24 was an original project, a starting point that the Swiss team could bring as a gift to its new union with BMW

SIDEPODS

The C24 was one of the most extreme cars as far as the shape of its sidepods was concerned, as they were concave in the lower area as can immediately be seen in the front view illustration, with a very high mouth almost of triangular shape. In the side view, take a good look at the height from the ground (1-2) of the mouth and the curious inclination forwards of the body in the upper area with, below, a knife edge zone that channels air towards the rear end. The barge boards behind the wheels were new and had small negative lift fins (3) of the Ferrari school.

Lack of an adequate budget restricted Sauber during its last season before the team was ceded to BMW, despite the car being very interesting on paper, Designed by Willy Rampf, the C24 comprised avant-garde features, like exhausts inclined forward and the sophisticated V radiator packs, already seen on the C23. However, the car was not given the required development, which would have meant the production of new moulds, even if the team had partially modified some components for almost every race. The key developments that took place during the season were seen at Melbourne, where there was a new front wing; Sepang, which yielded a middle wing above the rear light, which was further revised for subsequent races. The most important package made its debut at Imola and the different brake air intakes were first seen, while wings and vents were on the upper part of the sidepods together with new chimneys at Monaco. There were different turning vanes at Montreal and at Silverstone there appeared a front wing similar to that of Ferrari, as well as new barge boards behind the wheels that were also in Germany and Hungary, where maximum load wings also made their

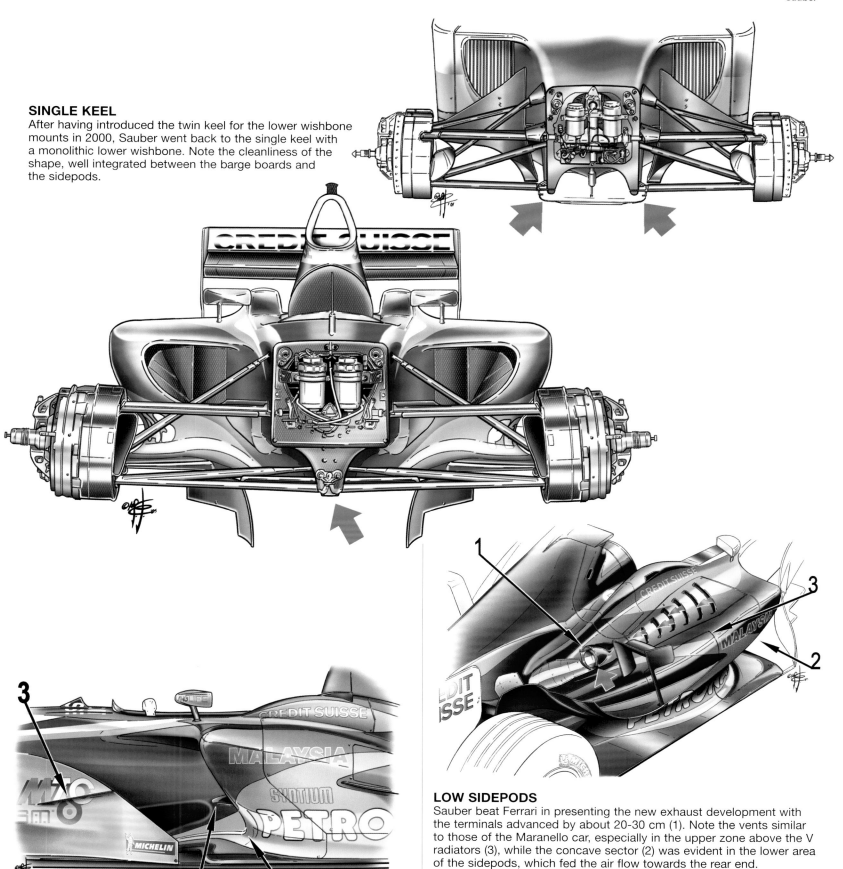

SINGLE KEEL

After having introduced the twin keel for the lower wishbone mounts in 2000, Sauber went back to the single keel with a monolithic lower wishbone. Note the cleanliness of the shape, well integrated between the barge boards and the sidepods.

LOW SIDEPODS

Sauber beat Ferrari in presenting the new exhaust development with the terminals advanced by about 20-30 cm (1). Note the vents similar to those of the Maranello car, especially in the upper zone above the V radiators (3), while the concave sector (2) was evident in the lower area of the sidepods, which fed the air flow towards the rear end.

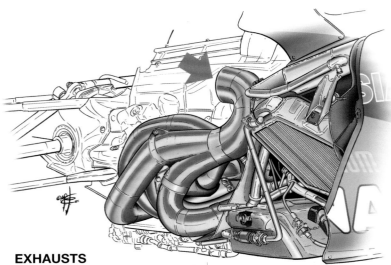

IMOLA
There was a new engine cover that was lower in the terminal area: a modification that can be easily seen from the greater exposition of the exhaust terminals, which were raised higher in the body, as can be seen from the comparison with the unit used until the Grand Prix of Bahrain.

EXHAUSTS
In detail, the new configuration of the forward inclined exhausts, which were debuted by Sauber. This is a feature developed at Maranello for the F2005. The terminals were advanced and, together with the sophisticated radiator layout, split and angled between each other; this technique enabled the team to produce particularly low sidepods.

DIFFUSER
The lateral channel (1) of the Sauber's diffuser was very sophisticated, with a curved zone near the wheel. There was then a single vertical fin (2), while the central channel had an Omega plane (3). To get around the norm that required less inclination of the lateral channels a large Gurney flap (4) then appeared. Note the extremely low position of the exhaust terminals (5) that exit well forward and close to each other at the centre.

NÜRBURGRING
Sauber came up with new chimneys, which were introduced only on the Saturday at Monaco. The shape was completely new in relation to the analogous solutions used by many teams and given a series of internal vertical vents, which had never previously been seen.

SILVERSTONE
Sauber was the only team to copy a feature first used by Ferrari – 50 cm wide overhanging mini-planes. They were only used on the Saturday at Silverstone because, despite the fact that they were determined during testing at Jerez, they were held up in customs at London until the Friday evening.

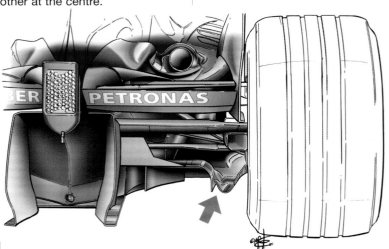

BUDAPEST

To obviate the tremendous heat, Sauber opened the chimneys it introduced at the Nurburgring (see circle) for the first time, and also abolished the small vents that were present on that occasion. But the volume of the first vent – indicated by the arrow – was notably increased of the series in the upper part of the sidepods

Nürburgring

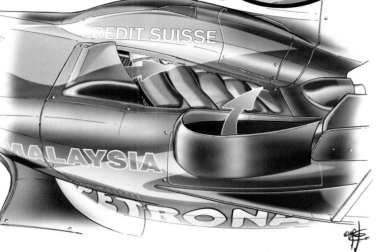

RADIATORS

The C24 retained an interesting and never previously seen radiator disposition that was inclined forward in V format, introduced on the C23 in 2004. Note the central cavity in the rear area in the rear area of the chassis, which contains the oil reservoir, like all the current F1 cars,

JORDAN

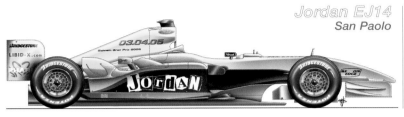

Jordan EJ14
San Paolo

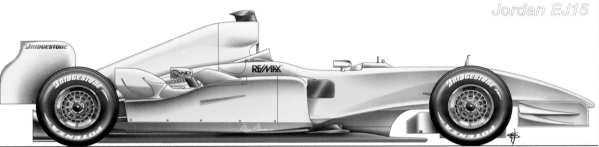

Jordan EJ15

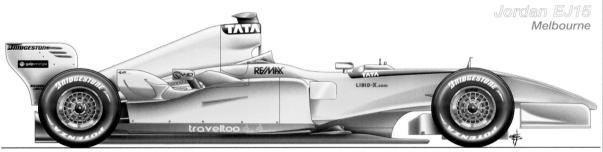

Jordan EJ15
Melbourne

Jordan EJ15 B

seen at Magny Cours had Sauber-type V-mounted radiators, which immediately created problems sufficient to force the team to revise the entire project and return in the mean time to a more traditional installation. The B version represented significant progress from the aerodynamics point of view, with the EJ15B finally able to develop good downforce without losing too much efficiency. The sidepods of the B were completely revised, as was the much tapered engine cover. One area in which the B showed notable progress compared to its predecessor was in overall weight.

The EJ14 could not even use a single kilogram of ballast, due both to the adoption of the lighter 10-cylinder Toyota engine and the progress made with the gearbox; weight was also saved with the various components to the point of being able to play with ballast to vary the weight distribution. The diffuser plane layout was very interesting, with new elements for the lateral channels.

REAR WING

Pre-season winter testing was carried out with this rear wing, which had end plates cut in their upper terminal area, a feature that was dropped from the first race in Australia. The new lower end plates were concave. The cuts in the upper part of the end plate near the leading edge were of the Toyota school.

A positive season for Jordan overall, having scored 12 points in the constructors' championship by the end of the season, especially if one considers that the team started the year with an intermediate car based on its 2004 chassis and gearbox and equipped with the new Toyota engine, which required a considerable amount of adaptation. There were two important moments for the team in 2005: the Grand Prix of Spain, when the lighter and more compact gearbox arrived, and the French GP when the B version made its first appearance, even if its real debut was then postponed to the Grand Prix of Hungary due to cooling problems. The car

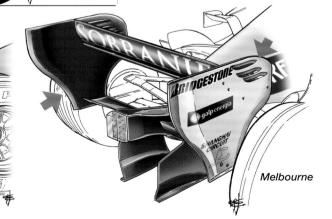

Melbourne

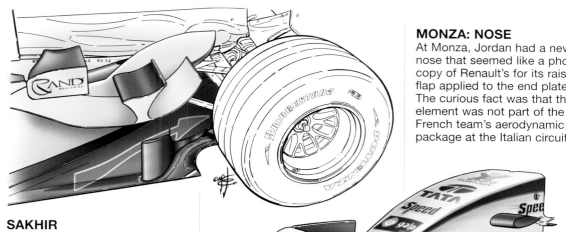

MONZA: NOSE
At Monza, Jordan had a new nose that seemed like a photocopy of Renault's for its raised flap applied to the end plates. The curious fact was that this element was not part of the French team's aerodynamic package at the Italian circuit.

REAR WING
Jordan was the only team at Monza to use a single plane in its rear wing, which was very similar to the one seen during the previous season. It was a good design in terms of aerodynamic load, but did not transmit a suitable level of stability to the car.

SAKHIR
Jordan also adopted these vertical fins in front of the rear wheels, introduced by Jaguar the previous season. Their purpose is to better channel air towards the rear of the car, screening it from the turbulence generated by the tyres.

SPA-FRANCORCHAMPS
Jordan introduced a new development in Belgium in which the diffuser plane was notably modified. Another with a chord of about 15 cm was fitted just above the lateral channels. A feature that obviously worked together with other planes in this zone and which favoured the extraction of air from the lower area of the lateral channels.

MAGNY COURS
The B version taken to France as the spare car was only used on the Friday. It had a modified chassis – note the different cut in its central area – (3) and the completely revised sidepods. The BAR school aerodynamic appendages were also new (1). The triangular fins were split in the upper area.

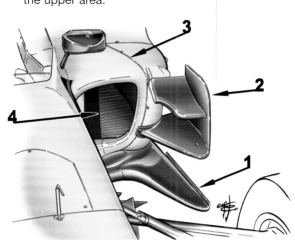

MINARDI

Minardi PS04B

Minardi PS05

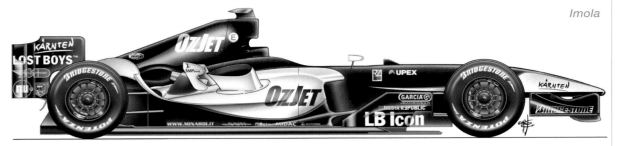

Imola

Imola, given the considerable amount of work carried out by the team to homologate two cars for the new season: the old car and the new PS05. So the new car was making its debut at Imola having covered just 200

sion for obvious cost reasons. The PS05 also underwent continuous development, with the introduction of new details at almost every race, until the Grand Prix of China. The 2005 season was the last for this team under the glorious name of Minardi, the Formula One career of which has been given a separate short chapter elsewhere in this book. Bought by Red Bull, the team is now called Toro Rosso.

IMOLA: PS05B SIDEPODS
The last new Minardi made its debut at Imola and was the work of engineer Tredozi. At last, it had a new concept chassis after three years during which the old unit had been substantially unchanged. The PS05 was an extreme car with innovative developments, such as a doubling of the planes in the small wings behind the chimneys. The position of the exhaust chimneys was also new as they exited in a more advanced zone near the car's body.

The season of Minardi, which was bought by Red Bull at the end of the year, finished with a flourish in that the PS05 had a wealth of vanguard technical content. Created by the working party led by engineer Gabriele Tredozi, the car did not make its debut until the fourth Grand Prix of the season at Imola and embodied a large volume of work: this was creditable, because the small Faenza team also had to complete modifications for the homologation of the 2004 season car, with which it competed in the early races of the season. The PS05 was the first Minardi of those that have competed in the last three seasons to have a new chassis and highly advanced aerodynamics, created in line with the latest fashion of sidepods that were extremely concave in the lower area. The car was almost a McLaren, conceived and built on

a tight budget: but it still comprised features inherited from its illustrious competitor. An extreme car in some ways, one of reduced dimensions even though with an unchanged wheelbase at 3,079 mm, tapered sidepods due to smaller radiators shaped lower and miniaturised mechanics designed around the 10-cylinder Ford engine, with its angle finally taken to 90° for a lower centre of gravity. The PS05's cast titanium gearbox was in its third evolution – a technology introduced by Minardi in 1999 – and was a gem of the car, which also had a rear suspension that was further refined in its basic layout. The main key characteristics of the PS05 were: more torsional rigidity combined with a reduction in weight – so much as to be able to take on no less than 50 kg of ballast on its debut – and vanguard aerodynamics. The new Minardi arrived in extremis at

test kilometres but was not in its definitive form. It was only at subsequent races that all the new components gradually arrived, the definitive version eventually bowing in at the Grand Prix of France. Having resolved initial problems with the clutch shaft, the car was reasonably reliable. Much work was done to lower the centre of gravity, moving all the weight of the electronic management systems in the lower area of the sidepods and working to rationalise cabling to the full. The only part inherited from the old car was the front suspen-

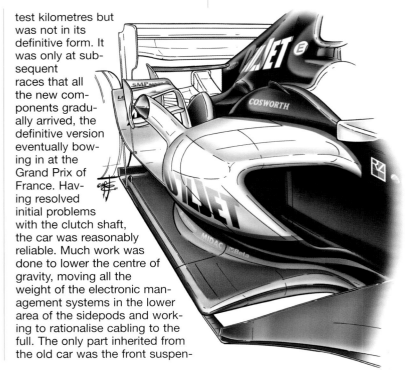

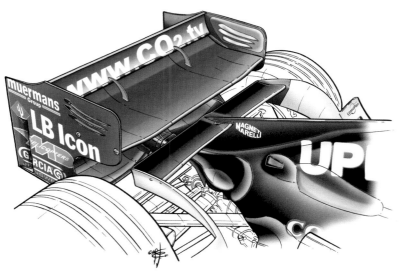

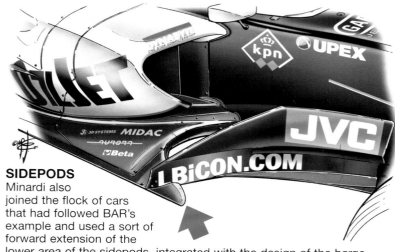

ISTANBUL: REAR WING

Apart from the new sidepods, Minardi retained the rear wing it introduced in Germany, characterised by a main plane of different heights (1) along its width. The end plates had both vents of the Toyota school (2) and the single vertical aperture (3), which appeared the previous year on the Minardi.

SIDEPODS

Minardi also joined the flock of cars that had followed BAR's example and used a sort of forward extension of the lower area of the sidepods, integrated with the design of the barge boards. A solution that permits better control of the air flow that feeds the lower area of the diffuser.

SAO PAOLO: FRONT WING

Minardi also followed Renault's example and joined the group of teams made up of Jordan and BAR in adopting the upper deck flap for the front wing. Introduced by the Faenza squad in Brazil, the feature was very similar to that of Renault, the flap forming a single element with the end plates.

SIDE VIEW

Designed by engineer Tredozi, the last Minardi was very clean and functional. Note the radiators with double inclination, the same as those of the Ferrari F2004 and the previous Minardi. The miniaturised rear suspension was very attractive, as was the latest generation gearbox in cast titanium and made by CRP of Modena.

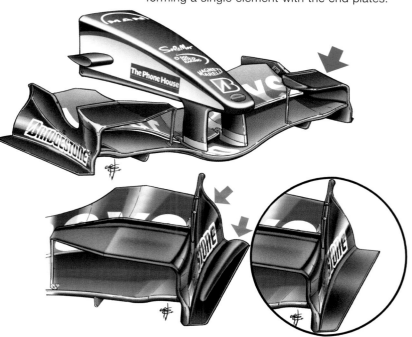

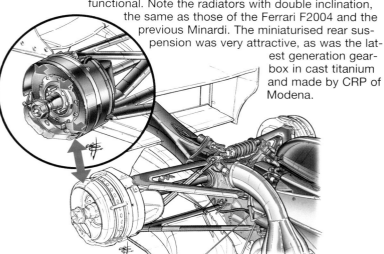

JAPAN

A further version of the new front wing, now with end plates with the first section flat and horizontal, but with an arched mini-channel.

REAR SUSPENSION

The layout of the rear suspension was practically unchanged, with the third transverse element given springs. Minardi was one of the first teams to follow the trend of completely fairing the upper area of the brake discs, expelling all the hot air from the open central area and so eliminating the "doughnuts" visible in the design of the old car – a technique launched in 2004 by McLaren

THE 2006 SEASON

Renault R26

McLaren MP4-21

Ferrari F248 F1

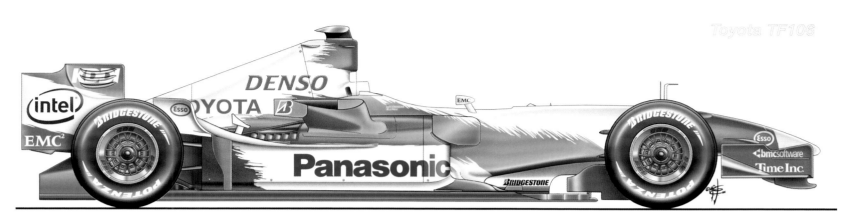

Toyota TF106

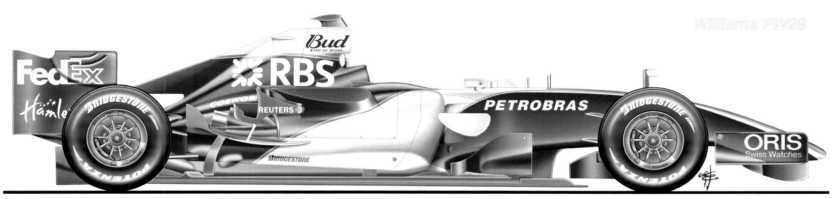

Williams FW28

Red Bull RB2

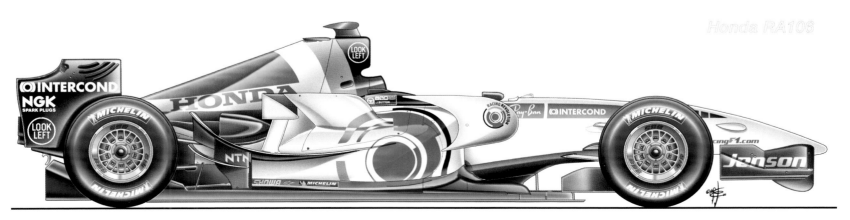

Honda RA106

BMW Sauber F106

Midland M16

Toro Rosso STR-01

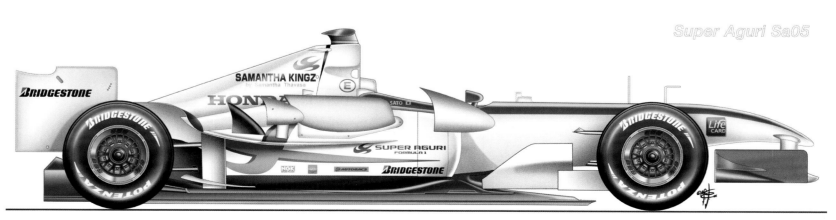

Super Aguri Sa05

REGULATIONS 2006

The 2006 season opened under the aegis of important new regulations. They concerned both the conduct of qualifying in an effort to provide more spectacle, and technical matters with the abandonment of the 3000 cc engine, introduced in 1995, for the 2.4-litre. Tyre changes during the races were also back: they became necessary in the light of the facts surrounding the 2005 Grand Prix of the United States of America at Indianapolis. But the most significant new technical rule for 2006 concerned the introduction of the new eight-cylinder engines, adopted by most teams due to the new regulations.

≃ **-10 cm**

ENGINE (ART. 5)

The new 2.4 litre cubic capacity and engines of eight-cylinders in the place of the 10-cylinders of recent years were the major new features of the 2006 regulations as they affected power units. Other changes concerned the angle of inclination of the cylinder banks, fixed at 90° for all teams, as was the minimum weight for the various engine components, equal to 95 kg. A maximum bore was also fixed at 98 mm and the distance between the cylinders of 106.5 mm.

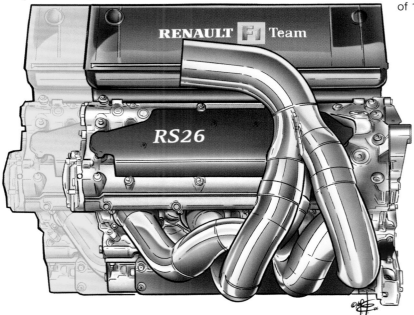

ART. 5.6

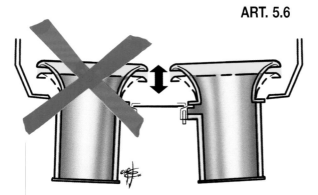

NO VARIABLE TRUMPETS (ART. 5.6)

Variable trumpets were also prohibited (Art.5.6), as was the variable geometry of the exhausts. The use of materials including magnesium and metalmatrix was also prohibited.

AERODYNAMICS (ART. 3.7.2)

The 2006 regulations imposed a notable limitation on the aerodynamic devices, especially in the front of the car. In an effort to avoid damage in the case of an accident and limit ground effect in the frontal zone, the various turning vanes located in an area starting at 330 mm above the front axle were placed at +40 mm in respect of the reference plane, while previously in the 50 cm central zone, they could rise up to the level of the reference plane itself.

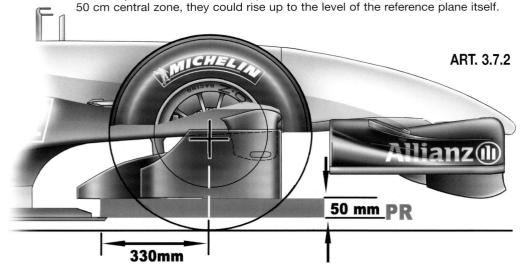

ART. 3.7.2

50 mm PR

330mm

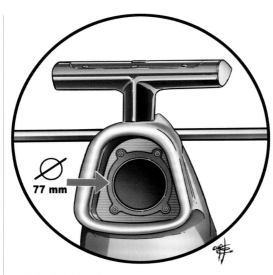

10 CYLINDERS

The smaller teams that had been unable to secure a supply of eight-cylinder engines were allowed to use the three-litre units of the previous season, but with the adoption of a 77 mm bottleneck flange and maximum revs limited to 16,700 rpm.

CRASH TEST (ART. 16.4)

Safety improvements were also brought in for the 2006 season, with the introduction of even more severe crash tests, especially for the rear of the car for which the maximum speed of impact went from 12 to 15 m/s. The deformable structure placed behind the gearbox could now push itself to 600 mm behind the rear axle - an increase of 100 mm - so as to ensure the necessary absorption of a blow, the compression of which had to be contained up to the height of the rear axle.

ART. 16.4

(v = 12 m/s)   v = 15m/s

R A
A P

780 kg

600mm
(500mm)

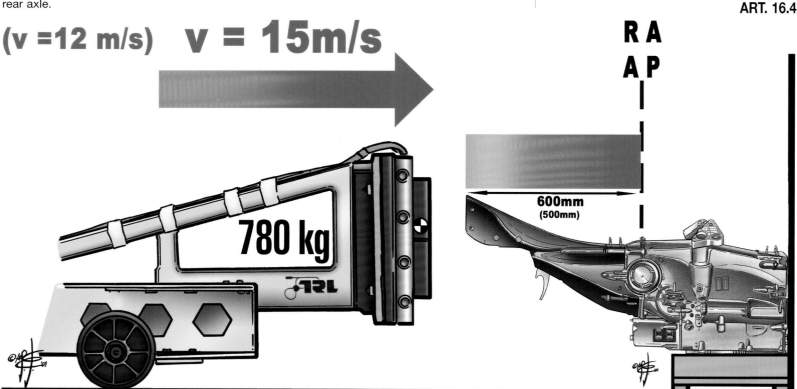

2006 SEASON

McLAREN-MERCEDES-BENZ

McLaren participated in testing before the start of the championship with its livery still coloured orange, which was a preview of the definitive version and its special fluorescent paint. The new MP4-21 retained its links with the MP4-20, even if its aerodynamics had become that much more extreme, with a narrower nose and more concave sidepods in the lower area. Of the previous car by Adrian Newey, who had moved to Red Bull in the meantime, there remained the curious "horn", which had not been adopted by any other team. The anchorage layout of the front suspension was also unchanged, fixed as it was directly to the chassis, a system that had, by that time, become common to the 2006 season cars.

RENAULT

Never touch a winning car! It is no coincidence that the R26 is the logical evolution that gave the French team its first world championship. The biggest new development was the engine, which had not only its cubic capacity and number of cylinders reduced, as required by the regulations, but now had a V 90° architecture instead of the V 75° of the old 10-cylinder. As far as the car is concerned, one thing to point out is the shape of the sidepods, which were even more concave in the lower area (the circle shows the 2005 car), but more than anything else the new philosophy that inspired the design of the new rear wing group, which had a central support and a plane heavily curved upwards in its central area.

FERRARI

Anyone who expected a revolution after the difficult 2005 season was disappointed: the new F248 F1 was not a complete break with the recent past, either as far as the dimensions of the wheelbase or the project's philosophy were concerned: they remained unchanged even if there were significant alterations to the aerodynamics. During the launch, however, many of the new developments were kept hidden, such as the new front wing and its doubled flap, and the elimination of the central step (on the right in the illustration). Instead, one was able to appreciate the rear wing, which had extremely sophisticated end plates. Ferrari is one of the few teams to have kept the single keel in the lower area of the chassis, to which the front suspension was anchored. The miniaturisation of the rear end was notable and had a new diffuser plane with an almost separate central channel.

TOYOTA

The TF106 did not drastically change the concepts already seen on the TF105, which were the revelation of the 2005 season. The nearest thing to an evolution of this car was the B version, which competed in the last two races of the championship with a new means of anchoring the front suspension, like that of McLaren. At Vallelunga just before the start of the season, a new and important aerodynamic step appeared that was not seen on the car that was at the official presentation and is shown in the illustration below. The front wing was new and had a supplementary mini-flap, new sidepods tapered in the lower area and rear aerodynamics all the elements of which had been revised, starting with the four small winglets located behind the engine air intake and completed by the diffuser plane

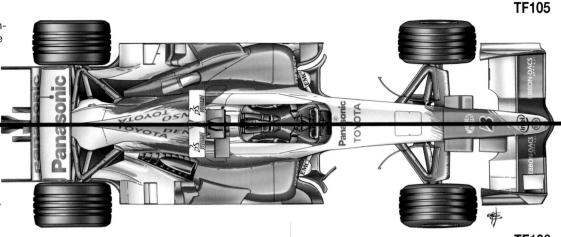

TF105

TF106
Barhain

RED BULL FERRARI

There were many new developments at Red Bull, starting with the supply of Ferrari engines in place of the Fords and concluding with the engagement of Adrian Newey. The car designed before the arrival of the ingenious British designer, whose departure from McLaren was a surprise development, retained the general shape of the RB1 one much different than that of the Newey cars. The most important new development was the adoption of the Renault-style tubular V keel with which to anchor the lower suspension. The illustration shows the initial area of the sidepods, which had been modified to improve cooling.

WILLIAMS-COSWORTH

The divorce from BMW and the agreement reached with Cosworth also coincided with the departure of Gavin Fisher, for many years responsible for the design of the Williams cars, so it was no coincidence that the new FW28 had few links with the British team's previous cars. The imposition by Loic Bigois, in charge of aerodynamics, became clear at first glance due to the more rounded and solid shape of the new car. Williams had also dropped the single keel in order to move on to the McLaren school split mount of the lower wishbone, down low on the chassis. The turning vanes behind the front wheels were the 2005 car's only legacy.

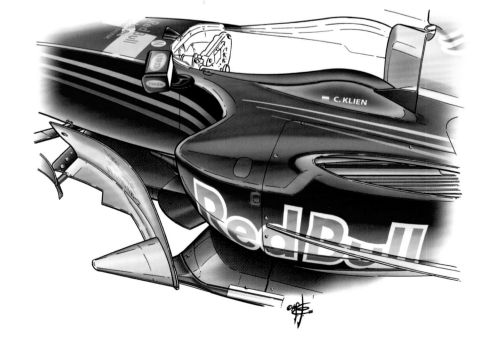

HONDA

The Japanese constructor registered a considerable improvement in quality, buying BAR at which, however, it retained the design staff; it was no coincidence that the new car was a natural evolution of its predecessor, created by Geoff Willis in 2005. Honda, too, had chosen to abolish the keel in the lower area of the chassis, modifying the shapes jointly to that of the nose as a consequence. The aerodynamic devices applied to the sidepods were taken to the extreme and had already been seen in embryonic form on the BAR 007. Notable improvements were made to the aerodynamics at the rear of the car, so that they became cleaner and more harmonious than those of the 2005 car.

TORO ROSSO

Instead of fielding the interesting car designed by engineer Gabriele Tredozi midway through the 2005 season, the heads of Toro Rosso preferred to compete with the old Red Bull car, almost without carrying out any significant modifications. The team was the only one to use an old 10-cylinder engine, with a 7 mm bottleneck flange and revolutions limited to 16,700 rpm, as required by the regulations.

BMW-SAUBER

After three fairly unlucky seasons with Williams, BMW took the considerable step of buying Sauber. Their new car took its inspiration from the concepts introduced during the previous season by Willy Rampf, who was retained as the technical head of the new team. The biggest difference between the previous year's car and the BMW-Sauber was the adoption of a layout without a keel, which was especially interesting in this case because Sauber was the team that introduced twin keels to F1 in 2000, having then moved on to a single keel and, finally, following the McLaren example.

SUPER AGURI

This is a kind of junior Honda team, which had acquired the 2002 Arrows cars and transformed them into eligible competitors for the 2006 season – an approach that created considerable perplexity, especially due to the little time available during the design stage. Super Aguri had, obviously, retained the extreme feature of twin keels, with the presence of two particularly long extensions with which to anchor the lower wishbone. A new nose similar to that of Renault made its debut on the cars in Bahrain.

MIDLAND

The new team was a continuation of the old Jordan and the new car took after the ex-B version that had been introduced mid-way through the previous season and of which it inherited many aspects. The agreement was renewed with Toyota for the supply of the new eight-cylinder engine in place of the old V10. Of clear Jordan descent were the aerodynamics, both in the front with the double barge boards inside the suspension, and the rear end, which had lateral diffusers with a second plane placed above it at mid-height.

THE LAST TIME FOR MINARDI AND JORDAN

Two relatively young but important names disappeared from the world of Formula One at the end of the 2005 season, Minardi and Jordan. The former made its debut in 1985 and competed in 340 Grands Prix; the latter first took to the F1 track in 1991 and contested 250 GPs: and both can look back on a history with a rich technical and sporting content. But only the British team came to know the joy of success, scoring four victories, one in 1998, two in 1999 and another in 2003, as well as an excellent third place in the 1999 Constructors' Championship. Always battling with sponsor problems, especially the Italian team, both made a notable contribution to the technical development of F1, especially Minardi. The Faenza-based team was an important presence in almost every edition of the Technical Analysis, coming out every season with developments that were often unique and were later copied by the other teams. One of them was the horizontal position of the rear brake calipers in 1999, later adopted for all the other cars in F1. The same goes for the 1995 spooned front wings that became an essential requirement, starting with the raising of the front wing in 2001, the year in which Jordan also led the way by taking up a similar solution. Minardi was also the first team to use titanium uprights, but even more significantly in 2000 it introduced a gearbox in the same cast material with the support of technological help from CRP of Modena, which then produced 'boxes adopted my many other teams, including Ferrari.

First the 1994 Minardi and then the 2000 Jordan used a step in the lower area of the sidepods, a refinement that has also been used in F1 in recent seasons.

The history of these two teams is peppered with the names of technicians and drivers of great talent. The 2005 world champion Fernando Alonso made his F1 debut with Minardi in 2001. Top engineers include Aldo Costa, the current Ferrari designer, who was chief technician at Minardi in the early Nineties, while Gabriele Tredozi, who is still the team's chief technician, even after it had changed its name Toro Rosso: he is considered one of the most creative and able designers in the sport. The last Minardi – the PS05 – was certainly one of the most interesting cars of the 2005 season: it was so innovative that it took its place right behind the top three of the sector. A real life fairy story took place under the Jordan banner: Gary Anderson, who was the chief mechanic in the days of the Emerson Fittipaldi McLarens, became a much respected designer. The first Jordan of 1991 was his creation and even today it is considered one of the most beautiful, simple and functional cars of the Nineties. The same can be said of the subsequent Jordan 194: it was powered by a Hart engine, which could not, unfortunately, compete with the best on the grid. As can be seen in the table in the appropriate chapter, it was always engine supply that was the weak point of these two teams, even if Jordan was able to use a works engine in the days of Peugeot.

MINARDI: A LITTLE HISTORY

Minardi joined the Formula One circus in 1985 with a couple of Ferrari designers, engineers Giacomo Caliri and Luigi Marmiroli, heads of Fly Studio; from the 1988 season, Caliri alone headed the technical team of the Faenza squad. A young engineer named Aldo Costa took his place in 1989 and he stayed with Minardi – assisted by Gustav Brunner in 1993 – until the end of 1995, when he joined Ferrari and was the head of the F2005 and 248F1 projects. Engineer Gabriele Tredozi took over at Minardi in 1996 and is still the technical boss of the team. Mauro Gennari worked with him in 1996/7, followed by Brunner again – he had worked at Ferrari in the meantime – in 1999/2000. In 2001, Tredozi was the lone technical director of the team, which changed its name to Toro Rosso from the start of the 2006 season.

HORIZONTAL BRAKES

In 1998, another feature introduced by Minardi was the horizontal rear brake calipers, which were first copied by Ferrari and then by all the other teams.

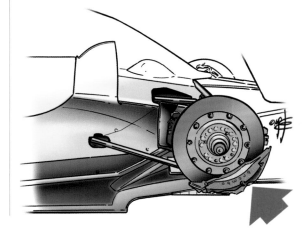

MINARDI ENGINES 1985-2005
Ford – in 1985, then alternating in 1988, 1989, 1990, 1993, 1996, 1998 and 1999;
Motori Moderni – 1985/7; Ferrari – 1991;
Lamborghini – 1992; Hart – 1997;
Fondmetal – 2000; European – 2001;
Asiatech – 2002; Cosworth – in 2003/5.

JORDAN ENGINES 1991-2005
Ford – 1991 and 2003/4; Yamaha – 1992;
Hart – 1993/4; Peugeot – 1995/7;
Mugen-Honda – 1998/9, 2000;
Honda – 2001/2; Toyota – 2003/5.

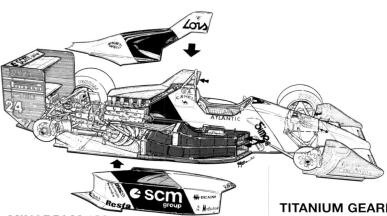

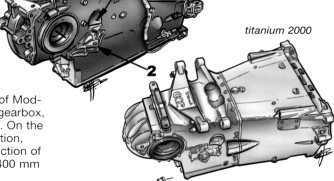

magnesium

titanium 2000

magnesium 2001

MINARDI M 189

The 1989 Minardi was the team's first car designed by Aldo Costa, assisted by Gustav Brunner. Costa continued to design the Faenza cars until 1995, the year he joined Ferrari.

TITANIUM GEARBOX

As a result of collaboration with CRP of Modena, Minardi installed a cast titanium gearbox, which was adopted by Ferrari in 2002. On the PS05 the 'box, now in its third generation, weighed little less than 12 kg – a reduction of 30% - and was not much more than 400 mm long.

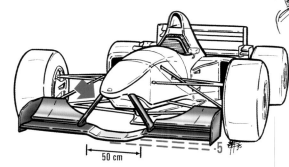

MINARDI M 194

This was the first car to have the step in the lower area of the sidepods, shown in the section below. It is a feature now used on all F1 cars.

INCLINED RADIATORS

In 2001, engineer Tredozi came up with radiators in an inclined position. This was a technique needed in order to start designing the more sophisticated positions used from 2002 by Ferrari and, subsequently, by other teams who went ahead with doubly inclined radiators to reduce the bulk of the sidepods.

MINARDI M 195

Back in 1995, Minardi introduced an unusual front wing, which was spoon shaped in the central area. A development that was adopted for all F1 cars after the limitations imposed by the regulations from 2001.

REAR SUSPENSION

Minardi also set the pace in this area, having become the first team to position their torsion bars (3) externally, with their dampers (1) inside the casting and linked to a transverse element. Later, the team adopted a layout with internal bars, which then spread to other cars (see the suspension chapter).

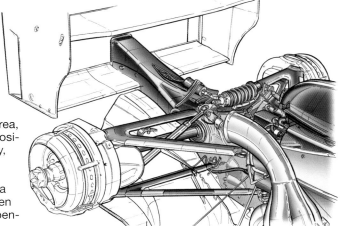

JORDAN: A LITTLE HISTORY
The British team came into Formula One in 1991 with Gary Anderson, who stayed with it until 1998, a season during which he was assisted by Mike Gascoyne, who took over the top technical spot in 1999. From 2000, Gascoyne was joined by Tim Holloway, who was then assisted by Egbhal Hammidy in 2001 before Gary Anderson's return for 2002/3.
In 2004, Nicolò Petrucci took over, in 2005 John McQuillam and James Key in 2006, when the team took on its new name of Midland.

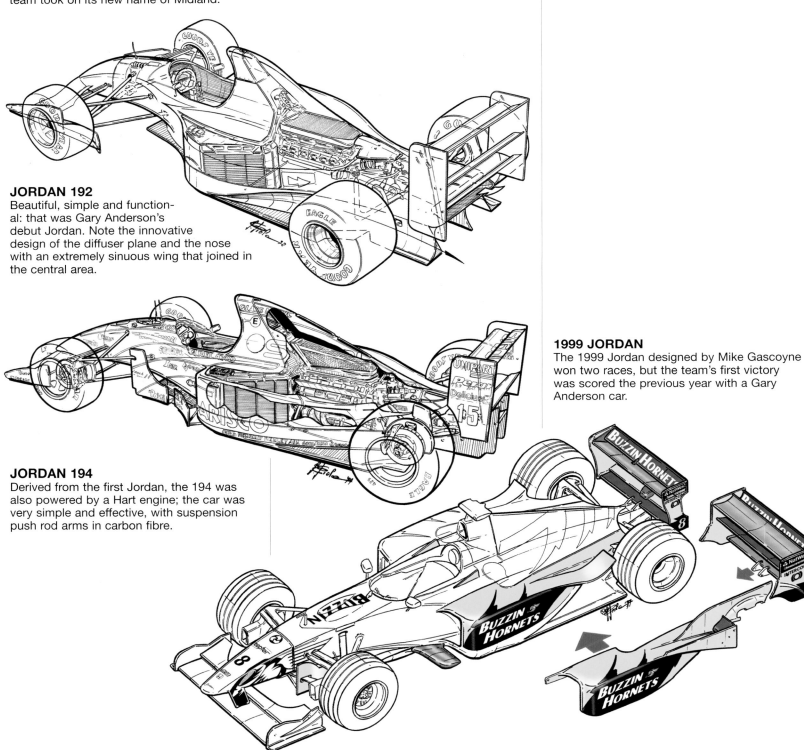

JORDAN 192
Beautiful, simple and functional: that was Gary Anderson's debut Jordan. Note the innovative design of the diffuser plane and the nose with an extremely sinuous wing that joined in the central area.

JORDAN 194
Derived from the first Jordan, the 194 was also powered by a Hart engine; the car was very simple and effective, with suspension push rod arms in carbon fibre.

1999 JORDAN
The 1999 Jordan designed by Mike Gascoyne won two races, but the team's first victory was scored the previous year with a Gary Anderson car.

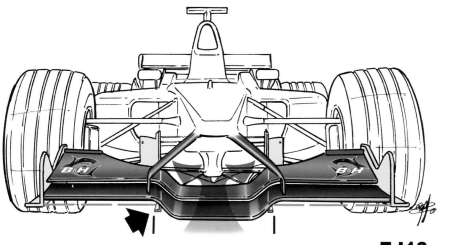

SPOON SHAPED WING

During the 2001 season, for which the regulations called for car noses to be raised 5 cm, Jordan led the way with this wing that was heavily stepped in the central area and had inverted V-shaped central supports.

JORDAN EJ13-12

Jordan adopted the twin keel suspension mount technique first used by Sauber, starting with an extreme interpretation on the EJ12 and then moving on to a more bland solution for the EJ13, which also had horizontal brake calipers on the front.

EJ 12

EJ13

EJ13

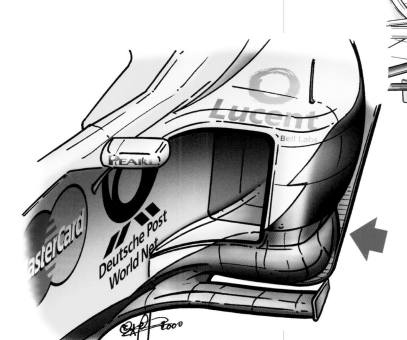

JORDAN EJ10

Jordan was the first team to bring back stepped sidepods, which were introduced by Minardi in 1994. It did so on the EJ10 from the 2000 Grand Prix of Germany.

JORDAN EJ14

Always a leader in front suspension, Jordan used split mounts of reduced height for the lower wishbone to better channel the air in the inferior area of the car.

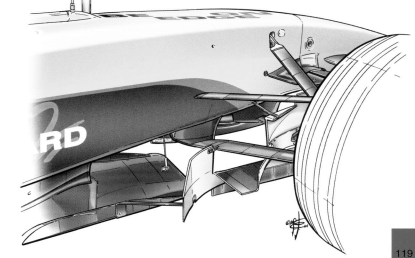

Giorgio Nada Editore S.r.l.

Editorial manager
Luciano Greggio

Editorial coordination
Leonardo Acerbi

Product development
Studio Enigma

Graphic design and cover
Aimone Bolliger

Translation
Robert Newman

Contributors
Mauro Forghieri e Mauro Coppini (engines)
Michele Merlino (engine table)
Mark Hughes (tyres)
James Allen (strategies)

Computer and graphic
Belinda Lucidi
Cristina Ravetta
Marco Verna
Gisella Nicosia
Alessia Bardino
Matteo Nobili

Printed in Italy by
Grafiche Flaminia S.r.l.
Sant'Eraclio (PG)
august 2006

© 2006 Giorgio Nada Editore, Vimodrone
    (Milano)

All right reserved.

*Apart from any fair dealing for the purpose of
private study, research, criticism or review, no
part of this publication may be reproduced,
stored in a retrieval system, or transmitted, by
any means, electronic, electrical, chemical,
mechanical, optical photocopying, recording
or otherwise, without prior written permission.
Allenquiries should be addressed to the
publisher:*

Allo stesso indirizzo può essere richiesto il
catalogo di tutte le opere pubblicate dalla
Casa Editrice.
*The catalogue of Giorgio Nada Editore
publications is available on request at the
address above.*

Giorgio Nada Editore
Via Claudio Treves,15/17
I - 20090 VIMODRONE MI
Tel. +39 02 27301126
Fax +39 02 27301454
E-mail: info@giorgionadaeditore.it
http://www.giorgionadaeditore.it

Formula 1 2005/2006 - technical analysis
ISBN: 88-7911-391-7